# INTERVIEWS OF JESUS

## Clarence E. Macartney

kregel
PUBLICATIONS

Grand Rapids, MI 49501

*Great Interviews of Jesus* by Clarence E. Macartney

Published in 1996 by Kregel Publications, a division of Kregel, Inc., P. O. Box 2607, Grand Rapids, MI 49501. Kregel Publications provides trusted, biblical publications for Christian growth and service. Your comments and suggestions are valued.

Cover Photograph: Copyright © 1996, Kregel Inc.
Cover and Book Design: Alan G. Hartman

**Library of Congress Cataloging-in-Publication Data**
Macartney, Clarence Edward Noble, 1879–1957
    Great interviews of Jesus / Clarence E. Macartney.
       p.  cm.
    Originally published: New York; Nashville: Abingdon-Cokesbury Press, 1944.
    1. Presbyterian Church—Sermons. 2. Sermons, American. 3. Jesus Christ—Friends and associates—Sermons. I. Title.
BX9178.M172G68    1996    232.9'5—dc20    95–32063
                                      CIP

ISBN 0-8254-3283-9

1  2  3  4  5  Printing / Year  00  99  98  97  96

*Printed in the United States of America*

# CONTENTS

Foreword . . . . . . . . . . . . . . . . . . . . . . . . . . . . . . . . 4

1. With a Murderer and Liar . . . . . . . . . . . . . . . . . . . . 5

2. With a Much-Married Woman . . . . . . . . . . . . . . . 17

3. With a Man Who Wore Chains . . . . . . . . . . . . . . . 29

4. With a Tree-Climbing Politician . . . . . . . . . . . . . . 38

5. With Two Dead Men . . . . . . . . . . . . . . . . . . . . . . 47

6. With a Harlot . . . . . . . . . . . . . . . . . . . . . . . . . . . . 56

7. With a Demoniac Boy and His Father . . . . . . . . . . . 65

8. With a Persecutor and Blasphemer . . . . . . . . . . . . . 73

9. With a Man They Could Not Hush . . . . . . . . . . . . . 82

10. With a Streetwalker . . . . . . . . . . . . . . . . . . . . . . . . 92

11. With a Judge . . . . . . . . . . . . . . . . . . . . . . . . . . . . 101

12. With a Man Who Knew What He Wanted . . . . . . . 112

13. With a Man Who Cursed Him . . . . . . . . . . . . . . . 120

14. With a Criminal . . . . . . . . . . . . . . . . . . . . . . . . . 128

15. With a Man on an Island . . . . . . . . . . . . . . . . . . . 137

# FOREWORD

M ost of the great utterances of Jesus were made in conversation with individuals. He did, indeed, on occasion preach to the multitudes, but the things which we remember best in His teachings were spoken in these personal interviews with men and women.

It is the personal touch and the personal word that counts, and here in these memorable interviews of Jesus we have that personal word and that personal touch. These interviews take in the whole ministry of Christ—heaven, earth, and hell. They strike every chord of human sorrow and temptation and sin and hope, and every chord, too, of the Gospel of grace and redemption.

CLARENCE EDWARD MACARTNEY

# 1

## WITH A MURDERER AND LIAR

He was a murderer. . . . He is a liar (John 8:44).

A murderer and a liar—that ought to settle the much-debated question as to the personality of Satan. You could hardly call an influence, an idea, an imagination, a figure of speech, or a personification a murderer and a liar. But that is what Jesus called Satan. Jesus said that he was a murderer from the beginning, that he is a liar and the father of lies. Either Christ Himself was a great deceiver or Satan is a personal power in rebellion against God, although under the government of God, and the great and subtle tempter and adversary of men's souls. When men see so much of evil and woe in the world, you can understand how they might debate about God, but the woe and sin and wickedness of the world certainly are all on the side of the existence of the Devil.

Carlyle took Emerson through Whitechapel, the terrible slums of London, happily not so terrible today, and then asked him after seeing those slums if he had any difficulty in believing in the Devil. In his brief but profound parable of the wheat and the tares Christ said, "An enemy hath done this," and then went on to explain that the enemy who is always sowing the tares where the wheat has been sown is the Devil. Men lightly dispose of Satan by calling him just an imagination of the mind, a figure of speech, a personification of evil. But what we want to know is, who is doing Satan's work in the world, mixing the fatal draught that poisons the hearts and brains of men? Who is it that dogs the steps of every toiling saint and digs pitfalls for his feet?

"The tempter came," says the evangelist. He is always coming. Standing in one of the great limestone caves in Bermuda, you can hear the flow of an underground stream. Those waters, ceaselessly flowing, have eroded the cavernous depths with their vast, resounding chambers and fantastic decorations. The mind reels as it tries to estimate how long that stream has been flowing. While empires have risen and fallen, while new continents have been discovered and added to the map of the world, while generation after generation of men have come and gone, strewing the earth with their dust, that stream which you now hear murmuring far beneath you has been flowing on and on, never interrupted, never ceasing, never getting through with its work; a symbol of the tireless energy of those forces in the natural world which make and unmake the seas and the continents. So temptation flows like a river through the life of man. Old races die out. New races take their place. New powers are discovered and new devices invented. But through every generation of mankind flows this river of temptation. It is as new as birth, as old as death. It touches the life of the fool and the philosopher, the prince and the pauper, the savage and the sage, Jesus and Judas. Wherever man has gone, temptation has gone. It is man's shadow, haunting him wherever he goes. It is the warfare from which there is no discharge.

Since Christ was truly man, He was in all points tempted like as we are. Here in this interview between Christ and the Devil, the most momentous interview in the history of the universe, we have the story of that temptation. The time of the temptation was immediately after His baptism by John and by the Holy Spirit. Then the heavens had been opened, and the voice of God had declared Jesus to be the Son of God. Immediately following this He was led—driven, Mark says—into the wilderness to be tempted of the Devil. Sometimes people are troubled about the petition of the Lord's Prayer, "Lead us not into temptation." How could God tempt us? they ask. Does not the Bible say elsewhere that God tempts no man? Yes; that is true. But it must be remembered that God is the ruler of our lives, and that in the providence of God we may be placed in circumstances where we shall be tempted. It was in the providence of God that Joseph was sold into Egypt, and by that same providence he was placed in the house of Potiphar, where he was subjected to his terrible temptation. Here Jesus, by God's appointment, finds Himself in the wilderness where He is tempted of the Devil.

The first temptation in the history of the human race took place in a garden and with man at peace with the whole animal creation. The temptation of Jesus, the second Adam, took place in a wilderness, where He "was with the wild beasts." That contrast between the first temptation and the temptation of Jesus, one in a garden, the other in a desert, is a picture of the ruin which had been wrought by sin.

The evangelist says He "was with the wild beasts." He had no human companion. Temptation is as lonely and solitary an experience, although as universal, as death. You cannot share it even with the nearest and the dearest. Other conflicts you can fight with comrades marching by your side, shoulder touching shoulder as you go into battle. But in this conflict you go alone. Satan never talks to ten men or to a company of men. He talks to one man. He singles him out from the crowd, draws him apart in the lonely wilderness, as it were, and then speaks to the soul. The scene of your temptation may be a crowded auditorium, a quiet study, a busy highway, or a country lane where the branches meet overhead. But wherever it is and whatever the circumstances, there you meet the adversary of your soul alone.

## THE TEMPTATION OF HUNGER

The Tempter came to Jesus when He was "ahungered" at the end of His forty days' fast. Satan knows when to come, when the opportune moment is. He did not tempt Jesus to turn stones into bread at the end of the first day of His fast, but when He was famished, when He was "ahungered." Hunger is one of the elemental appetites—with thirst, the strongest appetite of the body. Under the mad craving of hunger men have thrown off every consideration and refinement of civilization. The Bible tells us the story of those two mothers of Samaria who, when that city was besieged by Ben-hadad, made a pact to kill and eat first the babe of one mother and then the babe of the other. High up in the Sierras I once visited Donner Lake, a peaceful body of water nestling there under the mountains. But it was the scene of one of the most terrible tragedies in the history of the frontier. It was there that the stranded Donner party, on their way to California, were trapped in the mountain snows. These people represented the best American life, coming from the state of Illinois, but under the terrible drive of hunger they devoured one another. In one of those tales about our aviators floating in the Pacific on a raft, the narrator relates how they discussed the question of whether, if one of them expired, the others should eat his body. These facts show you the power of hunger. Jesus had a human body just like yours and mine; it was in the midst of His terrible hunger that the Devil came to Him and said, pointing to the round stones somewhat resembling loaves scattered over the desert, "If thou be the Son of God, command that these stones be made bread." The very mention of bread must have made the famished body of Jesus leap with desire.

Satan said, "*If* thou be the Son of God." Satan himself never doubted that Jesus was the Son of God. It was because he knew that Jesus was the Son of God that he tempted Him and tried to turn Him aside from His great work of redemption. Doubt as to the deity of Jesus is something that Satan left for churches and believers of this generation. What Satan was trying to do was to persuade Jesus to act in a way unworthy of His divine sonship. In the temptation there were two factors: the first the suggestion that Jesus gratify His hunger; the second the taunt that if He was really the Son of God, He could prove it by turning the stones into bread. In a sense it was the same temptation which Satan tried at the cross through the mouths of the passersby who mocked Jesus and reviled Him and said, "If thou be the Son of God, come down from the cross. If you are indeed the Son of God, surely it is not necessary for you to suffer; and you can relieve your sufferings and prove that you are the Son of God by coming down from the cross." But in neither instance did Jesus yield to Satan's temptation.

There was nothing sinful about turning stones into bread, and He had the power to do it, just as He turned water into wine; but to do so at the behest of Satan and to depart from God's present plan for Him would have been sin. Christ answered the temptation with the words from the book of Deuteronomy, "It is written, Man shall not live by bread alone, but by every word that proceedeth out of the mouth of God."

In His interview with Satan here, and in His refusal to do what Satan suggested to Him, Jesus is the sublime example for all those who in difficult circumstances are tempted to get out of those circumstances in a wrong way. The world says, "A man must live." That was the philosophy of Esau when he said, "What is my birthright to me when I am about to perish of hunger?" and sold it for a mess of pottage. "A man must live." God has given you the sex appetite; therefore indulge it. There can be no sin in it. That is what Satan said to Joseph: "A man must live. Yield to this temptation, and you will be favored and honored in Egypt, instead of going down into the pit of the dungeon." But Joseph answered, "A man must not live! A man must fear God. How can I do this great wickedness, and sin against God?"

"A man must live." That is what Satan said to the three Hebrew lads, Shadrach, Meshach, and Abed-nego, who were threatened with the fiery furnace if they did not bow down to Nebuchadnezzar's golden image. But they answered—and their great answer still stirs the souls of men—"O Nebuchadnezzar, if it be so, our God whom we serve, is able to deliver us. . . . But if not, be it known unto thee, O king, that we will not serve thy gods, nor worship the golden image which thou hast set up."

"A man must live." That is what Satan said to Daniel when he read the proclamation of Darius that for thirty days no prayers should be offered save to the king. "Say your prayers, Daniel, in your secret chamber," the Devil said to him. "Pray, but not at the open windows where your enemies can see you. Thus you can escape the lions' den." But Daniel said, "A man must not live, but his faith and trust in God must live." And three times a day, as his habit was, Daniel opened his windows toward Jerusalem and knelt down and prayed to the God of Abraham and Isaac and Jacob.

"A man must live," Satan said to Christ. "Yes," Christ answered, "but not by bread alone." A man must live, but not merely the animal man. The other man, the man of the heart, the man of the soul, must also live. It is written, written in the Word of God, written on the stars, written on the moral fabric of the universe, written on the heart and conscience of mankind, that man shall not live by bread alone, but by every word that proceeds out of the mouth of God. Tragic is that hour when the man who lives by the Word of God dies within you, and all that remains is animal and bestial.

## THE TEMPTATION OF PRIDE

Jesus has conquered the temptation of bodily appetite and hunger. Now the Devil tries Him on another side of His nature. Satan is not easily discouraged and not easily defeated. Christ has overcome Satan's first temptation by absolute reliance upon the will of God. Now the subtle Tempter, adapting himself to the circumstances, is going to tempt Him on that side of His reliance upon God. Satan takes Him to the pinnacle of the temple, one of the turrets of the huge structure built by Herod, rising six hundred feet about the valley of Jehoshaphat—"so high," says Josephus in his *Antiquities*, "that it made one giddy to look down from the pinnacle." The Devil can tempt a man in the wilderness and in the city, in the marketplace and in the church. Here he tempts Jesus at the temple.

From perhaps this very same pinnacle of the temple, some years later the brother of Jesus, James, was hurled to his death by the angry priests and Pharisees; for when they brought him up to the turret and commanded him to declare to the multitude below that Jesus was a liar and an impostor, instead of doing so James preached them a great sermon, calling upon them to repent and to believe on his crucified and risen Brother unto eternal life.

Here at the foot of the temple are visible all the collected glories of the throne of David. Here all the rivers of prophecy empty their streams, weighted down with the golden sands of inspiration. At such a moment, with such emotions stirring in the breast of Jesus, Satan says, "If thou be the Son of God, cast thyself down: for it is written, He shall give his angels charge concerning thee: and in their hands they shall bear thee up, lest at any time thou dash thy foot against a stone." Jesus has answered Satan's first temptation by saying, "It is written." Now Satan comes back with another "It is written" and quotes the beautiful passage of divine assurance and care from the ninety-first psalm.

> The devil can cite Scripture for his purpose.
> An evil soul producing holy witness
> Is like an illness with a smiling cheek,
> A goodly apple rotten at the heart:
> Oh, what a goodly outside falsehood hath.[1]

The proposal of Satan was that by casting Himself down from the pinnacle of the temple and then being rescued by the interposition of the angels, Christ would dazzle the multitude and, instead of taking the long, hard way of teaching and preaching and suffering persecution, would immediately, at the very beginning of His ministry, prove to everyone that He was the Messiah. But this temptation to pride, to make a show and a stir—and how that appeals to human nature!—Jesus scorned. He answered Satan with another "It is written"—this time, "Thou shalt not tempt the Lord thy God." Casting Himself down from the pinnacle of the temple to get recognition as the great Messiah was not God's plan for Him. God had indeed given that great promise with its spiritual implication, that the angels would bear Jesus up in their hands, and all others, too, who put their trust in Him. But it was not a promise that if He cast Himself from the pinnacle of the temple in a vain show to gratify pride He could count on the help of the angels.

How do men tempt and try God? They tempt God when they leave the appointed course of obedience and faith to go in the path of evil and temptation and then expect that they will be delivered. A man would not jump into the upper Niagara River and then expect that by some miracle God would keep

---

1. *The Merchant of Venice*, 1.3.

him from being swept over the falls. A man would not put a match to a keg of powder and then expect that God would keep him from being blown to atoms. And yet there are rational men and women who have, outwardly at least, turned away from evil and given their allegiance to God yet walk in the way of temptation and seem to expect that they will be delivered. When Augustine, shortly after his conversion, was accosted on the street by a former mistress of his sinful and licentious days, he turned and walked in the opposite direction. Surprised, the woman cried out, "Augustine, it is I!" But Augustine, proceeding on his way, cried back to her, "Yes, but it is not I." He meant that there was a new Augustine, and that this new Augustine would not tempt temptation by walking on the old territory of danger.

## THE TEMPTATION OF AMBITION

What is the most powerful temptation? According to Flaubert in his book *The Temptation of St. Anthony*, it is the temptation of the flesh. But if we are to judge from the climax of the temptations of our Lord, as we have the order of them in Matthew's gospel, then the most powerful temptation is the temptation of ambition. The Devil, having failed to tempt Jesus by hunger and by pride, now tempts Him by ambition. "The devil, taking him up into an high mountain, showed unto him all the kingdoms of the world in a moment of time. And the devil said unto him, All this power will I give thee, and the glory of them: for that is delivered unto me; and to whomsoever I will I give it. If thou, therefore, wilt worship me, all shall be thine." In a moment of time Nineveh, Babylon, Persia, Egypt, Greece, Rome, and all the world empires yet to come flash their pomp and splendor before the eye of Christ. All these kingdoms will be His *if* He will fall down and worship Satan.

Satan was lying, of course; for although great power has been permitted him and he is the prince of this world, yet the dominion belongs to God. But there was power and subtlety in the temptation. First of all, many of the rulers and conquerors of the world have attained their dominion by trampling the laws of God under foot and making evil their god. The history of mankind and of the kingdoms of the world appeared to be on the side of Satan's proposition. Second, the dominion of this world and its sovereignty had been promised to Christ. In the second Psalm God says to His Son, the Messiah, "Ask of me, and I shall give thee the nations for thine inheritance, and the uttermost parts of the earth for thy possession." Christ was to secure the kingdom, but it was to be by the path of loneliness, self-denial, suffering, agony, and death. His only earthly throne was to be the cross, His only earthly coronet the crown of thorns. Now the Devil tempts Him with an easier way, a short cut, to world dominion. But instead of asking it of God, He is to have it by asking it of the Devil.

In a moment of time Satan flashes all this glory, the splendor of Sesostris, Caesar, Alexander, Cyrus, and Nebuchadnezzar, before the mind of Christ. But in the same "moment of time" Jesus scorns the proposal. Here we have the climax of the audacity and blasphemy of evil, that Satan should throw off his disguise and boldly ask for the worship of Christ. Now, for the first time, Jesus denounces him as Satan, saying to him, "Get thee behind me, Satan: for it is written, Thou shalt worship the Lord thy God, and him only shalt thou serve."

In human life, this third temptation has its counterpart when men are tempted to secure what they desire or to hold what they possess at the price of compromise with evil, surrendering their principles, stifling their consciences—in short, bowing down to Satan. We see a great deal of that on the stage of world events. When Macbeth had his ambition stirred by the three witches, saw his opportunity to become king by assassinating his faithful lord, yet drew back from the dreadful crime, his more hardened wife read his letter hinting at his emotions and mused of him:

> Thou wouldst be great;
> Art thou without ambition, but without
> The illness should attend it.[2]

What is the illness which should attend worldly ambition?

---

2. *Macbeth*, 1.5.

It is a willingness and readiness to lower one's principle, silence one's conscience, and so bow down to Satan for the sake of securing some worldly aim. The Devil is always saying to men, "All these things will I give thee, if thou wilt fall down and worship me." Just a moment's bowing of the head, and the money, the office, the political prize, the business, the fame, shall be thine!

George Romney, the great English painter who used the beautiful Emma Hart, later Lady Hamilton, at whose feet Lord Nelson cast away his honor and his reputation, for a model of many of his beautiful paintings, such as "St. Cecilia," "Joan of Arc," and "Magdalene," deserted his wife and two children when a young man, having heard Sir Joshua Reynolds say that marriage spoiled an artist. During the years of his fame, he almost never saw his wife; but when at the end, old and broken in body and mind, he returned to her, she took him in and cared for him until his death. In "Romney's Remorse" Tennyson represents the forgiving wife as trying to cheer Romney with the thought that, although he had played a base part in the world, he had at least achieved greatness in his art:

> Take comfort, you have won the Painter's fame.

But Romney answers:

> The best in me that sees the worst in me,
> And groans to see it, finds no comfort there.

A man must always live with himself, and if the best in him must see the worst in him, then unhappy is that man. No comfort for him in fame, honor, riches, power.

During one of the political campaigns when the liquor question was an issue, a successful and popular pastor was invited out for a game of golf by two of his well-to-do parishioners. In a lonely place far down the course they turned aside from the game and told him they had asked him to come out and play with them so that they could talk with him about his attitude, and that of his church, in the current campaign. "We want you to keep silent on this subject," they said. The minister asked why. They answered that they were thinking of the welfare of the church. "We don't want you to say a word on this subject." The minister answered thus: "At the rate I am preaching and working, it won't be a great while before I have to retire. I shall be living on a small pension in a little cottage in some small town. But I must live with myself, and if I took the course that you men want me to take, I would be in hell a hundred times before I died." So Romney said, "The best in me sees the worst in me, and groans to see it."

Whenever and wherever a man agrees with the Devil and bows the knee to Satan, sad and dark is the overthrow and ruin of his soul. If there are guardian angels who follow the destinies of the soul and observe it at the turning points of life, then what must be their sorrow when they hear the soul agree to Satan's shameful terms. "What shall it profit a man, if he shall gain the whole world, and lose his own soul?" That question, it is important to note, was propounded by the only one who was ever offered the whole world and refused it. Alas, not for the whole world, but for one poor, paltry bit of its dust, for one soon-withering honor of the world, for one little moment of animal enjoyment, men will sell their souls!

As Christ was tempted "like as we are," so it is possible for us to overcome as He overcame. Christ did not resist and conquer Satan with divine power, save such as is available for you and me. When one of the old Scottish warriors going into battle saw that many of his soldiers had no breastplate such as he was wearing, he flung off his armor, thus showing to his soldiers that he would avail himself of no protection that they themselves did not have. So Christ fought Satan as you and I must fight.

One secret of Christ's victory was His *immediate* answer to the proposal of Satan. There was no parleying, no hesitation; immediately He refused the temptation, answering, "It is written!" Every time, also, He made use of the Bible and hurled a text of Scripture into the face of the Tempter. That same Word of God is our defense. So the psalmist said, "Thy word have I hid in mine heart, that I might not sin against thee." Christ won His victory by absolute reliance upon God. Archimedes, the man who said, "Give me a place on which to rest my lever and I will move the earth," is said to have destroyed the Roman fleet which was besieging Syracuse—where our Allied armies landed in Sicily—by setting them afire with the reflection of mirrors. An unarmed and weak mathematician destroyed the armada of a great nation because he put himself in touch with the forces of the physical universe. One unarmed and humble mortal can overthrow Satan and all his hosts if he will only put himself, and keep himself, in touch with that source of all spiritual power, the Lord Jesus Christ.

The most beautiful thing in this great interview, and in this great story, is the last thing. "Then the devil leaveth him, and behold, angels came and ministered unto him." Wonderful, glorious, blessed, and real angels! Still they come! Still they wait the issue of our battles! Still they minister their unspeakable comfort and joy to him who has refused to bow the knee to Satan and has remained faithful to God! When the angels come, angels of a good conscience, angels of self-respect, angels of heavenly fellowship, angels of the Savior's "Well done," then you know that the victory is worth all the long, hard struggle in the wilderness.

# 2

## WITH A MUCH-MARRIED WOMAN

The well is deep (John 4:11).

Some of the fondest and most stirring recollections of the Bible gather about its old wells. One of the earliest wells of which we hear was what we might call the Well of Providence. Hagar, the handmaiden of Sarah, driven out into the wilderness by the jealous anger of her mistress, fell down in despair and anguish on the face of the desert. But there God spoke to her and comforted her and showed her a well of water.

Another favorite well of the Bible is what we might call the Well of Romance. Traveling from the west, from Bethel, where he had seen the angels of God descending and ascending that ladder, the top of which reached to heaven, the fugitive Jacob came to a well in far-off Mesopotamia at the very time that the lovely Rachel came out to water her sheep. When Jacob saw her, he kissed her and lifted up his voice and wept. That was the Well of Romance. It is a well that is still used and, for some reason, never runs dry.

Another unforgettable well of the Bible is the Well of Bethlehem. During the days when he was a fugitive and outlaw, pursued by the gloomy and jealous Saul, David and his men found themselves hiding in a stronghold near Bethlehem, where David had been born. Lying under cover there, David began to think of his boyhood days, of his father and mother and those seven brothers, and then of the old well out of which he used to draw water for himself and for his sheep. As he thought of that well, a feeling of homesickness came over him, and David longed and said, "Oh, that one would give me drink of the water of the well of Bethlehem, which is by the gate!" Immediately some of his gallant followers hurried over to the well and brought him the water. But when David received it and realized that it had been secured at the risk of their lives, he would not drink it, but poured it out as an offering to the Lord. That well I call the Well of Memory. I have had men tell me how, when they went back after an absence of a quarter of a century or half a century to the old home where they were born, to the old farm on the hillside or in the valley, the first thing they did was to go around to the old well and drink again of its cool and refreshing waters. To them, that drink was a drink of old memories of childhood's joys, childhood's innocence, childhood's affection, and childhood's hopes, some of them, alas, already long since vanished and withered.

We come now to another well, the Well of Jacob, made immortal by the interview which Jesus had there with a woman of Samaria. The woman said to Jesus, "The well is deep." Twenty centuries before Jesus talked with her there, Jacob had dug the well and drunk thereof himself and his children and his cattle. Nearly twenty more centuries have passed since the day Jesus sat by the well and asked a drink of its water, and still the well is there, and still it is deep. On an August day—traveling, not as Jesus was from Judea to Galilee, but from Galilee to Judea—I paused in the heat of noonday at that same well and asked for a drink of water. Yes, the well is deep. But it is deep, too, in another sense; there is depth in the meaning of the wonderful interview which Jesus had there with a woman. It was deep for her; it is deep for us. As long as preachers preach, they will draw water out of this well; as long as souls thirst for something more than the water of this world, as long as men hunger and thirst after righteousness, they will draw water out of this old well. Now, with a sense of our need, let us ask for a drink out of this well which is still deep.

Jesus was on His way from Judea into Galilee, and the road led through Samaria. Some very straitlaced Jews who had to go to Galilee would take a long detour to the east across the Jordan and then to the north and then across the Jordan again to the west and so into Galilee, rather than defile themselves by passing through the country of the despised Samaritans. But Jesus was not troubled by such prejudices or bigotries. He and the disciples arrived at the village of Sychar, near the present town of Nablus, about noon. He and they were tired and hungry and thirsty. The disciples went off to the village to buy food, leaving Jesus by Himself at the well. John, one of the great painters of the Bible, gives us a wonderful portrait: "Jesus therefore, being wearied with his journey, sat thus on the well: and it was about the sixth hour."

There you can see Him resting by the well at the sixth hour, our noon, perhaps looking down into its cool depths where He could see an occasional gleam of the water far below, perhaps looking off toward those two mountains, Mount Ebal and Mount Gerizim, the Mount of Cursing and the Mount of Blessing, to which Joshua had appealed when, ages before, he addressed the assembly of Israel. The reverie of Jesus is disturbed by the sound of footsteps. Turning His head, He sees the woman of Samaria coming to the well to draw water, her earthen vessel gracefully poised on her head. That is very unusual, a woman coming to draw water at high noon. The time you see them drawing water in the Near East is in the early morning, before the heat of the day, or in the cool of the evening. The fact that this woman comes by herself and in the heat of the day shows an unhappy relationship with the women of her town. For her there is no friendly gossip and chatter of neighborly conversation as the women gather about the well. She comes alone in the heat of noonday.

## A Beautiful but Unhappy Woman

You and I never saw her. Perhaps we have never seen a painting of her, and yet she leaves a very definite impression upon our imagination. She is not young, and yet not old. There is undoubted grace and charm in her person and body as she moves quietly along, the vessel balanced on her head, her throat still full and round. In her face and person there are unmistakable

traces of beauty. We can be sure of that, for no woman without something of beauty could ever have attracted as many
men and husbands as she had. But there is something else
there, too, that is unmistakable—a look of sadness, weariness,
and disillusionment. It is a face from which expectation has
faded. The soul that looks out of her eyes is no longer expecting, no longer hoping for anything new or better or different.
And that is always a sad state to get into, when you cease to
look forward, when you no longer hope. "Hope springs eternal in the human breast." Does it? I doubt if that is so, for
every now and then I come in contact with one in whose
breast hope no longer springs. That is so of this woman.

As she draws nearer to the well, the woman reaches up with
her hand and, taking the vessel from her head, sets it down on
the stone parapet of the well, feeling embarrassed, perhaps,
because Jesus is sitting there. Looking up, Jesus says to the
woman, "Give me to drink."

Twice during His earthly ministry Jesus asked for a drink,
and both times the circumstances were such that we can never
forget the occasion. This was the first time, when He asked
this woman for a drink. The other time was when he hung in
agony on the cross and cried out, "I thirst." Then it was a
rough soldier who dipped a sponge in his sour wine and, putting it on the end of a reed, held it up to the parched lips of
the dying Savior.

Half in surprise and half in sarcasm or irony, the woman
says, "How is it that thou, being a Jew, askest drink of me,
which am a woman of Samaria?" It is as if she were saying,
"Well! This is a great surprise, to have one of the proud Jews,
who so despise the Samaritans, now ask one of them for a
drink." Jesus responds, "If thou knewest the gift of God, and
who it is that saith unto thee, Give me to drink; thou wouldest
have asked of him, and he would have given thee living water."
"If thou knewest the gift of God!" All things in life are the
gifts of God; but the supreme gift of God, which men so
disregard and ignore, is eternal life, that everlasting life about
which Jesus spoke to the woman. As the apostle said, "The gift
of God is eternal life."

## THE DIVINE MOMENT

Here is what you might call a wayside chance. It was not chance in the sense of accident, but chance in the sense of opportunity. Had the woman come a half hour earlier, she would have found the disciples there, and no interview would have taken place. Had she come at the ninth hour, at three o'clock, instead of twelve, Jesus would have been far on His way toward Galilee. But in the appointment of God she came at the sixth hour, at high noon, when Christ was alone, thirsty, and sitting thus by the well.

Jesus said to her, "If thou knewest who it is that saith unto thee, Give me to drink; thou wouldest have asked of him." How often our great opportunities meet us by the way, speak to us, plead with us, tarry for a little, and then, unrecognized, depart. "If thou knewest!" Think of that! If you knew how near God comes to you in His providences—in that joy that almost lifted you up to the sky, in that sorrow that almost plunged you into darkness and despair, in the piercings of conscience when it reproached you for some transgression, in the whisper of the Holy Spirit which called you to a higher life, in that mother who loved you and toiled for you, in that little child through whose eyes streamed the light of heaven, in that woman who loved you and cared for you. Oh, these lost chances, these opportunities to drink deep of the waters of peace and satisfaction! Too bad that so many never know these visitors from heaven until they are gone; then no pangs of regret, no tears, no entreaties, no prayers can call them back.

It is important, however, to remember here what Jesus said, and what He did not say. He did not say to the woman, "If thou *hadst* known." If He had said that, there would have been no hope for this woman. It would have meant that her opportunity had gone forever. On one occasion Jesus did say, and wept as He said it, "If thou hadst known." That was what He said to Jerusalem when He wept over the city: "If thou hadst known, even thou, at least in this thy day, the things which belong unto thy peace! but now they are hid from thine eyes." But to you and me Christ does not say, "If thou *hadst* known," but, "If thou knewest." Our great opportunity is still with us, and we can still ask Him to bless us and save us. How moving and how solemn that is—the fact that there are some of us to whom Christ now is saying, "If thou knewest," and to whom one day in the future He will say, as He said to the city over which He wept, "If thou hadst known the things which belong unto thy peace! but now they are hid from thine eyes." Lest you should be that one to whom Christ should so speak, hear Him now and call upon Him in this hour of opportunity. While He still speaks for you in the present tense, and not in the past tense, while He still says, "If thou knewest," not, "If thou hadst known," in repentance and in faith ask Him for the water of life.

EARTH'S WATER AND HEAVEN'S

Evidently somewhat puzzled by what Jesus had said about His giving her a drink and water that would leave her thirstless, the woman said, "How are you going to give me a drink? You have no vessel, no rope with which to lower it, and the well is deep. Our father Jacob dug this well and drank from it, and his children and his cattle. Are you better than Jacob? Do you know of a better well than this? Can you get water out of a deep well like this without drawing it?"

To this Jesus responded, "Whosoever shall drink of this water shall thirst again: but whosoever drinketh of the water that I shall give him shall never thirst." Thirst again! That is true of all waters, of all things in this life. They leave the soul with its deepest thirst unquenched. We drink here today, and tomorrow and tomorrow, like this woman of Samaria, with our empty vessel we must return and drink again. All the pleasures, all the achievements leave the soul with a something not yet tasted, a something beyond. There is something that the world cannot bestow. I remember a man who made this wise comment upon people of wealth and fashion who were pursuing the things of this world and forgetting the things of God. "They are trying," he said, "to get more out of this world than there is in it." How true that is. There is nothing in this world for the soul, and those who try to get out of the world lasting satisfactions for the soul are trying to get out of the world more than there is in it. Solomon found that out. He tells us of the great experiment that he made in women, in wine, in agriculture, in architecture, in statecraft. His verdict at the end was, "Vanity of vanities"; and, written or unwritten, that is the epitaph of every man who tries to get out of the world more than there is in it. The world cannot satisfy the soul because God has set eternity in the heart, and man is so constituted that he has an interminable longing after higher and greater things which only immortality itself and the greatness of immortality can ever satisfy. Only God can quench our thirst, the thirst that from the soul doth rise. "If any man thirst," said Jesus, "let him come unto me."

The woman is still puzzled by the words of Jesus. And yet it is plain that, however perplexed she may be by this strange talk of the water of life, she has now come to have full confidence in Christ. Perhaps she was asking for something more than just water when she said to Jesus, "Sir, give me this water, that I thirst not, neither come hither to draw." That at least she did ask for, a drink of this wonderful water, so that it would not be necessary for her to come every day at the hot noontide hour all the way from the village to draw water out of the well. "Sir, give me this water."

CHRIST AND CONSCIENCE

The next step, the next word, the next act in the stirring drama of this interview is one of the most dramatic things in the Bible. If someone had been telling you the story and you had never heard it before and the one who was telling it to you had got this far in it, had come to that request of the woman, "Sir, give me this water," you could never, never have imagined what the next word of Jesus, the next move in this strange drama would be. It was this: "Go, call thy husband." Husband! What had that to do with the water of life and with this woman's thirst? But Jesus moved quickly and wisely and with authority. "Call thy husband!" What was the purpose of that? It was to awaken her conscience, to reveal the woman to herself as a sinner. He was going to bestow a great gift on this woman, but no one can receive that gift until he feels his need. No one can take Christ as the Great Physician until he knows himself as sick. No one can take Christ as the Savior until he confesses himself as the sinner.

Now watch this woman. Her pale, still beautiful face flushes a little in surprise and embarrassment. "My husband! What has a husband to do with the water of life?" Instinctively, involuntarily, she throws up her guard—just as you and I would have done—to protect herself, to cover the secrets of her soul. "Husband!" she exclaims, her poise and assurance now recovered, "I have no husband." She means, of course, to lie, to deceive. But Jesus takes her words literally, as referring to the present, and in that sense what she has said is true. Jesus tells her, "Thou hast well said, I have no husband: for thou hast had five husbands; and he whom thou now hast is not thy husband: in that saidst thou truly." The woman has had five husbands, and probably the less said about her record with those five husbands the better, and now she is living in sin with a man who is not her husband.

"Go, call thy husband!" It costs something to be in the fellowship of Christ and to receive His greatest gift. That something is to part with every sin in our life. Jesus said to this woman at the well, "Go call thy husband." To another He may say, "Go call thy wife, whom thou hast wronged." To another, "Go call thy child, whom thou hast neglected." To another, "Go call thy father or mother." To another He says, "Go call thy bankbook." To another, "Go call the record of that business transaction." To another, "Go call that slander which you uttered against another's name." To another, "Go call that hatred or enmity which you treasure up in your heart." To another, "Go call that secret habit which stains and defiles thy soul." Can you meet these tests?

Without expressing the least indignation at the way Jesus had probed her soul and uncovered her past, the woman uttered no word of denial but said, half sadly, half hopefully, "Sir, I perceive that thou art a prophet." To call one a prophet was the highest tribute you could pay him. When the Pharisees asked the man born blind, whose sight Jesus had restored, what he had to say about the Man who had healed him, that was what he said: "He is a prophet." And that was what this woman said. Because Jesus knew all her past, how she had had five husbands and was living with another man who was not her husband, and because He could tell her all things that ever she had done, although He had never seen her before and had never talked with anyone else who had seen her, she knew that He was a prophet. That God knows and sees all is both a disturbing and a comforting thought. Sometimes when I talk with troubled and world-entangled souls and try to give counsel or advice, I cannot be sure as to the facts. How much, I wonder, in the life story of the one who talks with me is being kept back and hidden? But when we talk with Christ there can be utter frankness on our part, for He knows all. "He knew what was in man." We are on the way to improvement and to deliverance when we own and recognize that fact that Christ knows all that is in our heart. "O Lord, thou hast searched me, and known me."

## THE UNRECOGNIZED CHRIST

Disturbed now, and hoping to turn the conversation away from herself into more conventional channels, the woman asks the opinion of Jesus on a theological matter, the old dispute between the Jews and the Samaritans as to whose worship is the true worship. Pointing to the high mountain near by, she says, "Our fathers worshiped there, but you Jews say that Jerusalem is the only place to worship." Another than Jesus might have rebuked the woman and said, "Never mind that old dispute about the place of worship. What we are talking about now is your own heart, your own personal life." But Jesus accommodates Himself to her desire. He tells her that as between the Jews and the Samaritans, the Jews have the true manner of worship. Then He adds that great sentence, "God is a Spirit: and they that worship him must worship him in spirit and in truth."

God is a Spirit! This year the Protestant world celebrates the three hundredth anniversary of the adoption of the Westminster Standards of Faith. One of those Standards is the Shorter Catechism. When the committee in charge came to the question, "What is God?" they called upon one of their number to pray for divine guidance in answering that supreme question. They got their answer in the sentence of the prayer which the man then offered, an answer inspired by what Jesus said to the woman at the well, "God is a Spirit, infinite, eternal, and unchangeable in His being, wisdom, power, holiness, justice, goodness and truth."

"Ah, well," says the woman, "you may be right, and we Samaritans wrong; but one day Christ, the Messiah, will come, and he will settle the question for us, and settle it finally. When he is come, he will tell us all things." Jesus answers, "I that speak unto thee am he." Look now at that woman's face. This stranger who has talked so earnestly with her by the well and has asked her for a drink, He Himself is the Messiah! That then explains how He has made her heart burn within her. That is the secret of His knowledge about her past and present life. That is why He has awakened strange longings and deep thirst in her soul.

Before the woman could recover from her astonishment and before she could answer a word to that great announcement that He was none other than the Christ, the disciples appeared on the scene with the bread that they had bought in the village. Seeing them, the woman rose, and either in her hurry or in her embarrassment, or perhaps—who knows?—in the thrill of her new-found joy, forgot her waterpot and, departing from the well, went back to her village. The disciples, John tells us—and he was one of them—marveled to find their Master talking with a woman. Alone, too! And yet none of them asked Him why He did it or what it was He hoped to get out of a conversation with her. The brief comment of John, that the disciples "marveled that he talked with a woman," shows how Christ has changed the world.

Woman, who made it fit and decent and moral for a prophet to talk with you? Who threw a zone of mercy and protection about your little child? Who lifted you up and changed you from man's plaything to man's companion? Who changed you from man's chattel and property to man's friend and equal and inspirer? Who obliterated the brand of the slave from your face and put on your brow the halo of chivalry and tenderness and romance? Who so changed your lot that, instead of marveling today that a prophet should talk with a woman, what men marvel at is that there was ever a day when men should have marveled that Christ talked with a woman? Come, then, woman; break your alabaster box, filled with the ointment precious and very costly. Come, break your box and pour your ointment of love and gratitude upon His head and feet. Come, wash His feet with your tears of love and wipe them with your hair for a towel!

## THE FIRST WOMAN PREACHER

Back in her village, this once scorned and ostracized woman no longer avoided the men who were resting in the shade of the marketplace but went boldly to them and said, "Come, see a man, which told me all the things that ever I did: is not this the Christ?"

Moved by the eloquent sincerity of this woman, the first woman that ever preached the Gospel, the men hurried out to the well to see and talk with this wonderful person. Many came to Him because of what the woman had said, "He told me all things that ever I did!" That was a great and most unique sermon, for she did not tell what Christ had done for her, but how He had told her all the things that she herself had done. If Christ has told you what you have done, if He has told you, too, what you can do, then speak for Him as this woman did. Has He done nothing for you? Has He opened no sky of hope? showed you no hidden sins? given you no cup of joy and peace? Then hold your silence about Him. But, oh, if He has done something for you, if He has revealed Himself to you, if He has showed you how sweet His friendship is, how strong His arm is to keep you from falling, and how tender and kind He is to lift you up when you have fallen, then speak for Him as this woman did!

Perhaps the story of this familiar yet ever wonderful interview of Jesus with the woman of Samaria has reached and touched you with a sense of your own need. If there is any secret sin hidden in your breast, remember He has perfect knowledge of it. Nothing in your life is hid from Him. If as you have read this story and have heard Jesus say that if we drink of the water of this world we shall thirst again but that He can give us the water of everlasting life, you have said to yourself, "Yes; that is true. The things of this world can never satisfy me, and when I taste of them I always hunger and thirst again"; if the echo of His voice there by Jacob's old well has awakened in you hope where hope was all but dead, then call on Him; say now as that woman did, "Sir, give me this water."

> I heard the voice of Jesus say,
> "Behold, I freely give
>    The living water; thirsty one,
> Stoop down, and drink, and live."
>    I came to Jesus, and I drank
> Of that life-giving stream;
>    My thirst was quenched, my soul revived,
> And now I live in him.

# 3

## WITH A MAN WHO WORE CHAINS

He was kept bound with chains (Luke 8:29).

Memory paints vivid pictures on the tablets of the mind. Here is one of them: Four boys out on a camping expedition. Up one river and then up another. Supper by the campfire in a lonely ravine. At midnight a terrific thunderstorm. The boys take refuge from the storm in the haymow of a farmer's barn. Lying on the hay, safe now from pouring rain, they hear—when the thunder is not speaking—loud, wild cries of a human voice. All through the night they hear that terrible shouting. In the morning, when they come down from the haymow, they learn the reason. The farmer's father is insane, a maniac, and he is locked up like a dangerous bull or other animal in one of the outbuildings of the farm. Still the cries of the man echo in the memory of one of those boys. There were two storms that night: the storm of nature, the thunderstorm; and the storm of human nature, the storm of insanity in that poor man's mind and body.

Likewise there are two storms in the great story of Jesus' interview with a man who wore chains. First came the storm at sea when Jesus and the disciples were crossing over, and they awakened Him, thinking they were going to perish. And Jesus rebuked the wind and said to the sea, "Peace, be still." Then, after that storm and the quelling of the tempest, came the storm in a man's soul and the stilling of that tempest by the love and power of the Son of God.

There is nothing sadder than a wreck or ruin: the ruin of a house where the sacraments of love and marriage and birth and death have been celebrated; the ruin of a great city where the tides of life and business have once flowed, now scarred with flame, shattered by an earthquake, or devastated by bombs; the ruin of a primeval forest that has been swept by flames; the wreck of a great ship bound for a distant port and laden with a precious cargo, now broken on the rocks, with masts, sails, rudders, and boats all gone and the waves breaking over it with melancholy refrain; the wreck of a great palace or temple, where multitudes once came to salute their king or worship their God, now shattered and overthrown, nothing but a heap of rubbish where the lizards bask in the sun and the wild beasts make their lairs. But saddest of all is the wreck and ruin of a man, a human soul. All the ships on the seven seas might be sunk, all the beautiful buildings of the world reduced to rubbish, all the great cities of the world bombed and blasted, yet all that ruin could not compare with the ruin of a single soul made in the image of God. That is the pitiful ruin which we must contemplate now.

As soon as the boat had grounded on the beach and Jesus and the disciples had disembarked, they heard wild cries on the cliff above them. Looking up, they saw this dreadful wreck and ruin, this man or monster, rushing down toward them. His hair was long, matted, and disheveled; his body naked, gashed, and bleeding from the wounds made by the stones with which he had cut himself. On his ankles and on his wrists were fragments of the chains with which men had tried to bind him and which he had broken. In his face was a wild, maniacal look; yet with it all—and that was the infinite pathos and sorrow of it—the face of a man, made in the image of God.

The man belonged to one of the nearby villages. One day he began to act strangely; he said strange words, did strange things, had strange obsessions. The neighbors in town began to talk about him and wondered what his trouble was. Local remedies and traditional cures were tried. But the man was nothing bettered but rather grew worse. At length when he became violent and dangerous, they laid hands on him and bound him with heavy iron fetters, but in the strength and fury of his dementia he broke the chains as easily as Samson broke the ropes with which Delilah had bound him. Then, unable to cure him or secure him, the men of the town banded together and drove him out of the village into the country. There he took up his residence among the tombs, the caves dug out of the limestone cliffs which are still a feature of that part of the country and a striking corroboration of the truth of the narrative. There, in terrible anarchy and solitude, the outcast dwelt. Much of the time he was ranging over the mountains and hillsides, cutting himself with sharp stones, roaring and shouting day and night, frightening seamen whose ships came near the shore, and turning back travelers and merchants who wanted to pass that way. There the poor wreck and ruin lived—avoided, feared, abandoned—a picture of the isolation and devastation and loneliness of sin.

As soon as the disciples saw this monstrous-looking man and heard his cries as he came rushing down toward them, they laid hold on the boat and would have pushed out to sea again, preferring any storm that the sea could produce to the storm that was raging in the breast of the maniac. But Jesus had no fear. This wreck was His opportunity.

When the man came near to Jesus, he cried out—or rather the demons in him—"What have I to do with thee, Jesus, thou Son of God most high? I beseech thee, torment me not." But Jesus, standing His ground, said quietly to the maniac, "What is thy name?" In that question there was infinite tenderness and compassion. This poor wretched outcast, this wreck and hulk of a man, dreaded and avoided by his fellow men—in him Jesus saw one who was still a man, who was still a personality, and who had all the possibilities of manhood yet within him. The poor creature had a name among the sons of men, but he himself did not know what that name was or who or what he was. To the quiet inquiry of Jesus, "What is thy name?" the man gave a strange answer. You can see him standing there with the perplexed and troubled look on his face, as if some faint recollection out of the far past had come to him and then vanished. "My name? My name?" he seems to be saying to himself. "What is my name? Yes; once I had a name. Once father, mother, wife, child called me by my name. But now I have lost my name. I have no name." And then he cries out, "Yes; I have a name! My name is Legion, for we are many!"

Legion was the name of the Roman regiment. Many Roman soldiers had been buried in that country where their legions had been stationed to subdue the fierce barbarians. Not long ago a tomb was unearthed there with the name of a Roman soldier on it and the legion to which he belonged. Dwelling there among the tombs, the maniac had read those names and epitaphs. It may have been that one day he, too, had been drafted for one of the legions because of his great strength; that may have had something to do with his breakdown and ruin. Or it may have been that at the time of an uprising or rebellion in some town of Gadara he had witnessed the horror of death which the Roman legion left behind it—houses in smoking ruins, headless corpses strewn over the streets, the short Roman swords dripping with the blood of women and infants. Now all that horror comes back to him, and all that has befallen him seems to him as terrible as that. "Yes; I have a name! My name is Legion!"

You can see the disciples, still alarmed and frightened yet unwilling to leave Jesus by Himself in the presence of this monster. But they need not have feared for their Master. With the voice of unmistakable authority Jesus says, "Come out of the man!" At once a change comes over the wild man. The taut, tense muscles of his arms relax. The sharp, bloody stones drop from his hands. The wild look fades from his face; the look of reason, the look of humanity, the look of a man in the image of God takes its place. With a sigh of immense relief and deliverance as the demons depart from him, he sinks down at the feet of Jesus. One of the disciples wipes the blood from his face with a cloth, and another takes a mantle and casts it over his naked body. There he is, at the feet of Jesus, clothed and in his right mind. In the Bible we read of a number of persons who fell at the feet of Jesus: the woman who was a sinner and kissed His feet at Simon's feast; the blind, the dumb, the lame, the maimed who were laid at the feet of Jesus to be healed; Mary, the sister of Lazarus, who anointed His head and feet; Mary of Magdala, who fell at His feet in the garden; and John at Patmos, who fell at His feet as one dead when he saw Him standing in the midst of the seven golden candlesticks. But of all those great New Testament scenes there is not one which can compare with this: the poor demoniac whose troubles and sorrows were legion falling down at the feet of Jesus, clothed and in his right mind. Mighty, beautiful, sublime example of the power of Jesus to restore and redeem the human soul!

## THE DEMONS' REQUEST

In this great interview and in this great miracle there is a series of three requests—only one of them refused, the very one we might have expected Jesus to grant. The first request was that of the demons. On the steep hillside nearby there was a herd of swine feeding, two thousand of them, with the herders watching them. The demons said, "Send us into the swine!" That is the most dreadful prayer ever uttered. Who can measure the horror of it? These demons were fallen angels. After Christ Himself they were by nature next in the universe. What a tragedy Spirits once bright and fair at God's right hand now asking permission to take up their abode with the beasts that wallow in the mire.

"Send us into the swine!" Alas, how often that petition is repeated by men made in the image of God. Whenever I see men pouring liquor into their bodies, whenever I see them swarming around the doors of a filthy show, whenever I see them bound for some place of wicked entertainment, I hear again that dreadful petition, "Send us into the swine!"

To this request Jesus gives His consent. But even the hogs are unhappy and miserable with the demons in them, which shows that mankind, alas, can sink to lower depths than that of the beast. The swineherds, sitting together with staves in their hands, jump to their feet when they see the hogs leave off grazing, run around in circles, and start toward the sea where the cliff is so steep that their momentum will carry them over irresistibly. The swineherds run among them, trying to head them off, striking them over the head with their cudgels, but all in vain. Over the cliff in a mad rush and stampede they go, two thousand of them, and the whole herd is drowned in the sea.

Unbelievers have often debated over the catastrophe which befell the swine. Once, sitting in my study in the town where I had my first church, I remember an infidel painter on his ladder plying the pious house owner with the difficult question about the destruction of that herd of swine—not the possibility of it, but whether or not it was right for Christ by His command or permission to let the property of these Gadarenes be destroyed. But Christ Himself gives us the answer in another place. "How much then is a man better than a sheep?" Here He says, "How much is a man better than a hog? What matters if two thousand hogs are drowned, but a soul is set free from the cruel dominion of Satan?"

THE SWINE OWNERS' REQUEST

This brings us to the second request, that of the owners of the swine. The swineherds, as soon as they saw the drowning of the hogs, ran to the town and told everyone what had taken place. Just as people rush today to see a wreck or a fire or any other disaster, so the people of the town rushed out of their homes and over the fields and hills and down to the edge of the cliff, where they saw some of the drowned swine already floating on the surface of the sea. Then they went over to where the man whom Christ had healed was sitting at the feet of Jesus. When they had seen and heard all, they made their sad and ungracious request. "They began to pray him to depart out of their coasts." In healing the possessed man Jesus had conferred a great blessing not only upon him but upon the whole community by delivering them from the fear of the wild maniac who had always threatened their lives. But they had cared nothing for that. All they could think of was the loss of their hogs. They besought Him that He would depart out of their coasts.

Jesus does not go in where He is not wanted. It was He who said, "Behold, I stand at the door, and knock: if any man hear my voice, and open the door, I will come in to him, and will sup with him, and he with me." But He does not force His way in. He might have brought great blessings to those people of Gadara, but they asked Him to depart out of their coasts, and He departed.

Have you ever asked Christ to depart from you? Do you fear that His shadow might fall across your ledger or cast a damper over your entertainment or make you uncomfortable in some friendship? Do you fear that if He did not depart, He might look upon some secret chamber in your life to which you dare not admit Him? Yes; that request of the owners of the swine still echoes through the world today.

## THE HEALED MAN'S REQUEST

Now comes the third request, the request of the man who had been healed. The two requests come one after the other, but how different they are. The first asks that He depart out of their coasts; the other asks that Jesus permit the man whom He has healed to remain with Him. The man so recently healed no doubt wanted full opportunity to show His love and gratitude to Christ. Perhaps, too, there was the dread lest, if he were parted from his new-found master, that old and terrible master, Legion, would again claim him. Then he saw the angry and cruel faces of the owners of the swine. He would have to live among them, and he would always be pointed out as the man who had been responsible for the loss of their livestock. No wonder the man felt safer in the presence of Jesus. But this request, so beautiful and natural, is the one that Jesus refused. He granted the request of the demons that they enter into the swine. He granted the request of the swine owners that He depart out of their coasts. But the request of this grateful man whom He had healed He refused. He told him, "Return to thine own house, and show how great things God hath done unto thee." That meant that the man could be more useful telling of Christ in his own home and among his own people than he could be traveling about with Christ. It meant, too, that like the rest of us the man had to walk by faith and not by sight. It meant that the presence and power of Christ through the Holy Spirit and through our faith in Him is as real as His bodily presence. Here Christ put the man's duty above the man's desire, beautiful though that desire was.

A man who had been converted at one of Spurgeon's services came to him after the meeting and expressed the desire to go out and do Christian work. Spurgeon looked at him and said, "What are you?" the man answered, "I am an engine driver." "Is the stoker a Christian?" said Spurgeon. "No," the man answered. "Then, there, in your engine, with the stoker working at your side, is your field of duty and opportunity."

I can see the former maniac standing there on the cliff watching Jesus and His disciples as they get into the boat and start across the lake. The horizontal sail is raised. The wind fills it, and soon the ship is sailing rapidly westward toward Capernaum. The man watches until the ship is just a blur on the horizon; then he turns and goes back toward his village.

When the shepherds see him coming, they run off their flocks, calling one to another, "Get your flock into the fold! Legion is coming!" When he gets near to the outskirts of the town, the boys who have been playing run headlong, shouting to one another, "Run for your lives! Legion is coming!" When the people of the town hear the cry, the shops are emptied; mothers run out into the street and drag in their children. Every window is barred, every door bolted, and even the growling dogs take refuge under the houses. When he arrives in the town, it is like a city of the dead; not a person can be seen. But his daughter, opening the door an inch or two and looking out, cries to her mother, "Mother, it is Father! But he has his clothes on, and his face is not covered with blood, and there are no broken chains on his arms or legs, and instead of leaping over the ditches and dikes he is coming straight down the road!" Then the mother looks out, and when he arrives before their home, she and the children open the door and rush out to greet their father. Quickly the word is passed up and down the street. One by one the doors and windows open, and soon all the inhabitants gather about Legion as he stands there in front of his house and in the midst of his family, clothed and in his right mind, ordained a preacher by Jesus Himself, and tells them the great things that Christ has done for him and how the Master has had compassion upon him.

Here is a man who has been translated from the power of Satan unto God. Men still debate about evil spirits and how they can possess a human soul. When I see what goes on in the world as reported in the morning newspaper, I have no difficulty whatever on that score. I see what men do and what they become when possessed by the evil spirits of drink and lust and hatred and anger and jealousy. I am not troubled by a narrative like this. The same Christ who healed this man is still able to save to the uttermost them that come to Him. The evil spirits in this poor man could not be bound, no, not with chains. But there he is now, sitting at the feet of Jesus, clothed and in his right mind! To every evil spirit, to every evil habit, to every temptation, to every sorrow, to every fear, Christ is still able to say, "Come out of him."

> He breaks the power of canceled sin,
> He sets the prisoner free.

What will you ask of Jesus? Will you ask Him to depart from you? Will you say that again, as you have said so many times before? Or will you say, "Lord Jesus, come into my heart"?

# 4

## WITH A TREE-CLIMBING POLITICIAN

*Zacchaeus, make haste and come (Luke 19:5).*

In the days when the tax collectors were robbing the people in France, a party of Parisians were amusing themselves by telling stories of great robbers. One of the company was Voltaire. After listening quietly to some of the tales of notorious thieves, Voltaire said, "I can tell a robber story better than any of yours." The whole company was instantly quiet, waiting for the words which were to fall from the lips of the chief figure of the literary world at that time. Clearing his throat, Voltaire began as follows: "Once upon a time there was a tax collector, a former general." Then he was silent. The others present at once called for him to continue. "Why do you stop? Go on! Let us hear the story of your greatest robber." Whereupon Voltaire said, "I have told you the story. Do you not see that my statement about a tax collector implies the greatest robber story in history?"

If in Jerusalem or Jericho or Samaria or Capernaum a man had aroused the curiosity of his friends by announcing to them that he was going to tell them the story of the greatest robber and then had commenced, "Once upon a time there was a chief publican," he would have had to proceed no further, for everybody would have understood what he meant. The great robbers of Christ's day were not those who infested the high-ways, like the thieves in the story of the good Samaritan, but the tax collectors, known as publicans. The Roman government required a certain per capita tax from all the people. It farmed out the business of collecting taxes to chief publicans, who in turn farmed it out to the publicans. The chief publican had to pay the Roman government the required per capita tax, and he could keep for himself as much more as he could squeeze out of the people. The Jews looked with great abhorrence upon the business of the publican, especially when he happened to be a Jew, regarding him as a traitor to his people. His business was thought of as odious and nefarious. No decent person would associate with a publican. The name was synonymous with sinner and criminal—hence the common saying, "Publicans and sinners." The bad business in which the publican was engaged and the hatred and contempt in which he was held by the populace reacted upon his own character and gave him a heart as hard as a grindstone. It was bad enough to be a publican, still worse to be a chief publican, and that is what the man of this story was. He was a chief publican, and, like all of them, he was rich with his ill-gotten gains.

The name of the chief publican was Zacchaeus. That is important to remember, because it means "pure" or "innocent." The man was far from pure or innocent, as we shall see. But the beauty of the story is that his meeting with Christ restored him to his better self. The soil and stain were rubbed off his name, and it stood forth again in all its clearness and beauty.

Jericho, far down from Jerusalem, on the edge of the plain of the river Jordan and the Dead Sea, was supposed to be a cursed city; for Joshua, when he had destroyed Jericho at the time of the conquest of Canaan, had pronounced a curse on anyone who attempted to rebuild it. That curse had been fulfilled centuries afterward in the death of the first-born of the man who first rebuilt the city. But others had persisted, and Jericho was now a large and prosperous town. It may have been a cursed city in the minds of the people, but there arrived that day in Jericho one who was able to turn a curse into a blessing. Two men there would never forget that day when

Jesus came to Jericho. One was a blind man and the other was a short man. One was a beggar, the other was a very rich man. But Christ blessed both of them forever and ever.

This is how it happened. Jesus was on His way up to Jerusalem, where, before long, He was to be crucified. That adds something to the story, because Zacchaeus was one of the last men whom Jesus called to Him before He was put to death. On the bright spring morning when Jesus came to town, Zacchaeus was sitting on the veranda of the imposing house which he had built with the money of extortion. He may have had a tablet in his hand, estimating how great his wealth was. Presently he heard a stir on the street before him and, looking up, saw first the little boys, always in the front of the crowd, running down the street. After them came the people, some walking, some running, all gesticulating and talking excitedly. Wondering what it meant, Zacchaeus called one of his servants and said to him, "What is the excitement? What are all the people running for?" The servant answered, "Jesus of Nazareth is passing by! Jesus is coming to town today!"

## CURIOSITY

Jesus of Nazareth! The chief publican had often heard that name. He was the chief personality then in all parts of Judea and Galilee. If General MacArthur were to come to town tomorrow, all the stores and offices would be emptied, and the streets and windows would be filled with people curious to see the man who has stirred the hearts of the American people as they have not been stirred for many a year. Human nature is the same from age to age. It is not strange, therefore, that the crowds were running to secure a place of vantage where they could have a good look at Jesus as He passed through their town.

Although he was a hardened publican, Zacchaeus had a natural and commendable curiosity and "sought to see Jesus who he was." It is not possible to tell all that was back of that saying of Luke, "to see who he was." Was it just a natural curiosity to see a notable person? It was that, at least. But perhaps there was something more in it. Who knows but that Zacchaeus had not been altogether happy with his robberies and extortions? Who knows but that the better man within him was longing for something higher and nobler? No doubt he had heard of Matthew, another publican—indeed perhaps he knew him—who had been taken into the band of disciples by Jesus. Evidently, then, Jesus thought that there was something good in a publican after all.

Whatever his thoughts, Zacchaeus flung aside his financial sheet and, gathering his fine linen robe about him, left his house and ran down the street with the rest of the people. But when he arrived at the place where Jesus was going to pass, he found the crowd lined up in front of him. Being a man of short stature, he was not able to see over them. Since he was a hated and scorned publican, the people in front of him made sure that he could not see between them or pass in front of them. Sometimes, however, a disadvantage turns out to be an advantage, and a handicap may be a real help. It was so here. The fact that he was short of stature and could not see over the shoulders of the crowd only served to make Zacchaeus all the more determined to see Jesus who He was. In front of him was a sycamore tree, what they speak of in the Eastern countries as a plane tree, one of those large and gracious trees which are the benediction of the Near East. How often have I myself, faint and weary in following the footsteps of St. Paul, sat down beneath one of those plane trees and solaced my soul in its grateful shade.

Zacchaeus acted quickly. Reaching up to one of the low, overhanging limbs, he agilely pulled himself up into the tree and climbed from branch to branch until he found the very top.

I imagine that a good deal of ridicule and abuse followed Zacchaeus as he climbed up to his perch. Probably that was how Jesus learned his name, as some of the people shouted with derision after him. One said to another, "There goes that old publican and extortioner, Zacchaeus, whose heart is as hard as a grindstone. He is the robber of widows and orphans. May he burn in Gehenna forever." Some of the street urchins, too, probably threw a rock or two at him as he climbed to the top of the tree. But Zacchaeus cared for none of these things. You will never get anywhere in the world or amount to anything in life or see any of your dreams or ambitions fulfilled if you are going to be frightened and turned back by criticism and ridicule and opposition. Zacchaeus, the short man, wanted to see Jesus, and there he was up in the top of the sycamore tree with a better view than any of the crowd below him on the street.

Presently the procession of which Jesus and His disciples were a part drew near to the tree, the boys as usual running ahead of the crowd and chattering shrilly one to another. And now came the one who had so stirred the city. But how meek and lowly He was! No banners, no trumpets, no insignia of rank about Him, and after Him came the twelve ordinary-looking men, fishermen and peasants, one of them a publican just like Zacchaeus.

When Jesus was opposite the tree where Zacchaeus had taken his observation post, He came to a standstill and, looking up into the tree, saw Zacchaeus. It would seem as if He had been looking for him. There is an old tradition, and a very beautiful one too, that when Matthew the publican was received into the band of the disciples, he said one day to Jesus, "Master, if you ever go through Jericho, I hope you will look up an old friend of mine, the chief publican there, Zacchaeus."

Whether He had been told of Zacchaeus in advance or whether by divine intuition, He knew his name, his need, and where he was at that moment. Jesus paused and said, "Zacchaeus, make haste, and come down; for today I must abide at thy house." Zacchaeus could not have been more surprised if that sycamore tree itself had talked to him. The great Prophet and Healer had stopped and spoken to him and called him by name, and, more than that, He had invited Himself to dine with Zacchaeus, an outcast, a hated publican, and a sinner.

This was one of those divinely appointed turning points in the history of a soul, when the soul and its opportunity meet. Perhaps there are others for whom Jesus is looking and to whom He is now calling; they too have come to the turning point, and if they obey the voice of Christ and come, they will enter into eternal life.

Jesus said, "Make haste!" Immediately the great hope sprang

up in the heart of Zacchaeus, and without a moment's delay he let himself down out of the tree, breaking off leaves and branches in his hasty descent, while the crowd looked on in amazement. Bowing before Jesus, he conducted Him down the street to his own mansion. When the people who were following saw that Jesus was actually going into the house of Zacchaeus, they were astonished; and they murmured to one another, saying, "What do you think of that? He calls Himself a prophet, and yet He is actually going to dine with Zacchaeus, a publican and a sinner! How shocking! I never felt sure about Him anyway, whether He was a real prophet or not. Now I am sure He is not, for no real prophet would ever sit down at the table with Zacchaeus." But here as always, Jesus, who was seeking and saving the lost, was indifferent to the opinion of others and made Himself of no reputation.

REPENTANCE

The evangelist does not tell us what Jesus said to Zacchaeus during that dinner. No doubt He spoke earnestly to him about the way of eternal life. The crowd which had gathered outside could not see or hear what was going on, but after the dinner was over, Luke says Zacchaeus stood, evidently where the people now could see him and hear him, and said to the Lord, "Behold, Lord, the half of my goods I give to the poor; and if I have taken anything from any man by false accusation, I restore him fourfold."

The Jewish law and custom required that a man should give the tenth of his income to the Lord. And the more Christianity a man has in him today, the more he will strive to equal and even to surpass that requirement of the old dispensation. Zacchaeus showed that his repentance and conversion were sincere because he determined first of all that, where it was possible, he would make restitution to anyone whom he had robbed and, second, that he would give not a tenth but the half of his goods to the poor. People sometimes hesitate to embrace Christianity and come into the church lest it cost them something, or lest they must give up this or that worldly pleasure. But when you have genuine repentance like that of

Zacchaeus, it is not a question of, What will I be required to give up? but, What can I give to my Lord who sought me and found me?

Some of the most memorable sayings of Jesus came out of personal interviews with individuals. The great statement about regeneration and new birth, "Ye must be born again," came out of His nocturnal interview with Nicodemus. The great statement about the water of life, of which if a man drink he shall never thirst, came out of His memorable interview with the woman at the well of Samaria. And out of this interview with Zacchaeus came that immortal saying which sums up the whole mission and work of the son of God upon the earth through the ages, "The Son of man is come to seek and to save that which was lost."

KINDNESS

The sycamore tree into which Zacchaeus climbed that spring day at Jericho so that he might see Jesus has become one of the greatest pulpits in the history of the church. It preaches, first of all, a sermon on the power of kindness. That was how Christ won Zacchaeus. Suppose He had paused under that tree and, looking up at Zacchaeus, had called out to him, "You child of the devil! You who grind the face of the poor and turn orphans and widows out on the street, how shall you escape the damnation of hell?" Now Jesus knew how to condemn and how to be severe. In language far beyond that which I have just imagined Him speaking He denounced and excoriated and anathematized the evildoer. But here was a man who was still capable of being won for God. If Jesus had denounced him in those words I have just used, you and I would never have heard of Zacchaeus. Instead of that, He spoke kindly to him and called him to come down and went to his house as a guest.

You know that old fable of the wind and the sun. They once had a debate as to which first could make a man take off his cloak. First the wind tried it. It stormed and raged and blew. But the man only wrapped his mantle the closer about him as he cowered before the blast. Then when the wind had given up, the sun shone kindly and warmly upon the man, until, heated by its rays, he divested himself of his garment. We can all take the method of the sun. We can all take the method of the Savior that day when He dealt so kindly with the outcast publican and brought out the best that was in him and made the name Zacchaeus, which means "pure," but which was soiled and darkened and obscured by sin, stand forth again in its original meaning.

> Down in the human heart,
> Crushed by the tempter,
>   Feelings lie buried that grace can restore;
> Touched by a loving heart,
>   Wakened by kindness,
> Chords that were broken will vibrate once more.

## JOY

The sycamore tree preaches, in the second place, the joy of receiving Christ. He did not come to make you heavy and solemn and sad. He came that your joy might be full. And the highest and purest of all joys is the joy of receiving Christ into your heart. There is no joy in all the range of human or super-human angelic experience which is comparable to that. Even the angels themselves are envious with a holy envy when they see a soul receiving Christ into it; although, as unfallen creatures, they cannot know that joy of repentance and faith and salvation, they do the next best thing possible—rejoice over one sinner that repents. Do you know the joy of Zacchaeus? Whatever you miss in this life, oh, do not miss this highest and purest of all joys!

## OPPORTUNITY

The third thing to remember is that when his chance came, Zacchaeus acted quickly. Christ said, "Zacchaeus, make haste." Zacchaeus did not delay a moment. He made haste and came down. Suppose he had said, "Well, I will wait until I can go to Him when there are not so many people looking on," or, "I'll get a little further information about Him first." If so Zacchaeus would never have found Christ, for that was his last opportunity, his first and his last. Jesus was on His way up to Jerusalem. Never again did He pass through Jericho.

During the past summer when climbing a great mountain, one of the highest of the peaks of Southern California, about halfway up we came to a pure mountain stream. All about it were abundant grass and ferns and bracken. In the green stretches under the trees beneath us we saw many deer feeding at the eventide. Just where the trail crossed the stream there stood a post with a board nailed to it, and on the post these words were painted: "Last water." This was to warn the traveler that here was his last opportunity to get a drink, fill his canteen, and water his horse. Between that stream and the summit of the mountain there was no water.

Last water! I have often thought of it since. Last water! Last water! The last opportunity to do some friend an act of kindness! Last water! The last chance to speak the word of regret or reconciliation! Last water! The last chance to break the chains of an evil habit! Last water! The last opportunity to repent and to come to God.

Again Jesus of Nazareth passes by. Would you not like to see Him, who He is and what He can do for you? Would you not like to share in the wonderful joy of Zacchaeus that day when he came down out of the tree and received Jesus into his home and into his heart forever and ever?

# 5

## WITH TWO DEAD MEN

There talked with him two men, which were Moses and Elias (Luke 9:30).

Three summers ago I climbed with my brothers the highest mountain of the San Bernardino range in California, San Gorgonio. From the barren, rock-strewn summit of that mountain we commanded a magnificent panorama: toward the south the desert and the Salton Sea, toward the east endless waves of brown mountains rolling toward the Arizona desert, to the west and north the checkered squares of the orange orchards and the vast Pacific. The view was one of great uplift and inspiration, well worth the long, hard ride up the winding trail. But we had no thought of remaining on the top of the mountain, even for a single day. A high mountain is not a place to live. You go up to the top of it to get the view, to feel the uplift of that view amid silence broken only by an occasional sigh of the wind, like the sigh of time itself, as you look out over the handiwork of God. So it is with the Mount of Transfiguration. It is not a mount on the top of which you stay, as Peter wanted to do when he suggested that they build there three tabernacles, one for Moses, one for Elijah, and one for Jesus. It is for us, as it was for Christ Himself and for His three disciples, a mount of vision, of uplift, of comfort, of faith confirmed—and then back to the work of life.

The Transfiguration, which receives so prominent a place in three of the Gospels, is not often spoken of in Christian

47

teaching and preaching. The hymn writers have memorialized all the other events in the ministry of our Lord, but I know of just one hymn on the Transfiguration. And yet, although not in the sense that Peter meant it, it is "good for us to be here," and it will be with profit and inspiration that we climb this mountain.

Because the confession of Peter in answer to the question of Jesus, "Who do men say that I the Son of man am?" was made just a little while before this at Caesarea Philippi, near snow-clad Mount Hermon, the great mountain in that part of the world, some are quite certain that it was on Mount Hermon that the Transfiguration took place. But the more traditional Christian site is Mount Tabor, which rises abruptly out of the plain of Esdraelon, and at the foot of which Deborah and Barak won their victory over the myriad hosts of Sisera.

On this memorable evening Jesus took with Him three of His disciples, Peter and James and John. They had been honored similarly once before, when He took them with Him into the death chamber of the daughter of Jairus. They were to be so honored once again, although unworthy of it, when He took them with Him into the innermost recesses of Gethsemane when He entered into His agony. We can only conjecture why these three disciples were chosen. We know that they were strong and leading men among the twelve. All of them were to profit, too, by the experience of that night when they saw their Lord transfigured. Peter would need the memory of that glory when he was overtaken with craven fear, and John would need the memory of it when he was in prison on Patmos, and James would need the memory of it when he laid his head on Herod's gory block. Long afterward, Peter wrote how he and the other disciples had seen the Lord's glory and had heard the voice on the mount saying, "This is my beloved Son, in whom I am well pleased."

There is nothing in the narrative which mentions the time of the Transfiguration, but it has always been assumed that it was at night. Leaving the nine other disciples in the village at the foot of the mountain, Jesus and His three friends climbed slowly up the steep side of Tabor, until at length the villages and the broad plain below were just dark spots in the distance.

Then the stars came out, and the wind from the Mediterranean, the south wind, so fresh and grateful in all that country, began to blow. It was night when earth received her Lord at Bethlehem. It was night, at least a supernatural night, when Christ died on Calvary. It was just between the night and the morning that He left His grave in Joseph of Arimathaea's garden. And here, when He was transfigured, it was night.

When they reached the summit of the mountain, the three disciples, evidently exhausted with the climb, sank immediately into sleep. But while they were sleeping, Jesus was praying, and "as he prayed, the fashion of his countenance was altered, and his raiment was white and glistening." When the disciples awoke out of their untimely slumber, they saw Him in His glory and the two men, Moses and Elijah, also in glorious array, who talked with Him. To Peter the whole thing seemed so wonderful that he wanted to stay there, build three tabernacles, and so retain the heavenly visitors on the mount. But before any answer was made to his impulsive request, a cloud overshadowed them, and the disciples heard a voice saying, "This is my beloved Son, in whom I am well pleased; hear ye him." At that the disciples were sore afraid and fell on their faces on the ground. But Jesus came and, touching them, said, "Arise, and be not afraid." When at length they dared to lift up their eyes, they saw no man "save Jesus only." Elijah was gone. Moses was gone. The cloud was gone. The soul-shaking voice was gone. Only Jesus, with His familiar voice and His familiar appearance, was left.

## THE PURPOSE OF THE TRANSFIGURATION

The purpose of the Transfiguration must have been to strengthen and comfort and encourage Jesus as He drew near to His death and work of redemption on the cross. The purpose cannot have been to impress the disciples with a great overwhelming spectacle, although that spectacle, as we have seen, made a deep impression upon them and must have influenced their lives to the very end. The clue to the meaning of the Transfiguration is found in the fact that it followed by only a few days the announcement by Jesus of His approaching death.

Just after Peter made his confession at Caesarea Philippi, Jesus began "to show unto his disciples, how that he must go unto Jerusalem, and suffer many things of the elders and chief priests and scribes, and be killed, and be raised again the third day." Just as when He entered into His agony in Gethsemane and confronted the cup that He must drink for the world's salvation, Jesus here wanted both human and divine sympathy and companionship. That was why He took Peter and James and John with Him into the innermost place of Gethsemane and asked them to watch and pray with Him; and that, I am sure, was the chief reason that He took them with Him to the Mount of Transfiguration.

Even though the divine glory of Christ's personality was for a moment unveiled here on the mount, we must not forget His complete humanity, for He was in all points tempted like as we are, yet without sin. One of the natural and inevitable temptations of life is the shrinking from death. As Jesus contemplated the last dread experience, so close at hand, He went up to the mountain to pray, in order to fortify His soul against that hour and that trial; and in His struggle and distress He wanted the presence and the sympathy and help of Peter and James and John. The disciples failed Him here, as they did in Gethsemane, for as soon as they reached the top of the mountain, they fell asleep. But the Father did not fail Him. God never fails those who earnestly pray to Him and wait upon Him.

We do not know what words Jesus uttered in His prayer on the mountain. Perhaps it was the same prayer that He was to utter with bloody sweat in Gethsemane, "If it be possible, let this cup pass from me." If so, we may be sure that He made the same condition at the end, throwing Himself completely upon the divine will, "Nevertheless not as I will, but as thou wilt." It was *as* He prayed, Luke tells us, that "the fashion of His countenance was altered, and His raiment was white and glistening."

In a true although in a different sense of course, prayer, earnest heartfelt prayer, transfigures the face of the man who prays. Someone sent me recently a painting of a little child in a forest with her basket of flowers by her side, her face glowing as she kneels devoutly before a wilderness shrine. And I shall never forget a visit I made to the cathedral at Strasbourg, with its world-famous clock—the procession of the twelve apostles passing before Christ every day at noon and four allegorical figures striking the quarter hours, a child, a youth, an old man, and finally Death itself. The vast nave was empty when we entered that day. Far in the distance at the high altar we could see the dim lights and hear the murmur of a priest's voice. As we stood listening and watching, an elderly gentleman, clad in sober black, and a beautiful child of perhaps seven years, with hair as yellow as gold and eyes as blue as heaven, came in and knelt on the stone flags just in front of us, their heads reverently bowed and their hands clasped together as they adored the Savior of the world. I saw wonderful paintings that summer and other summers in the great cathedrals of Europe—paintings by Rembrandt, Murillo, Velasquez, Titian, El Greco, Rubens, Raphael—but this was by all odds the finest picture I saw, the beautiful child and the old man kneeling side by side before the mystery of Christ and Him crucified. For the old man, life was mostly in the past. He had tasted its joys, seen its beguiling and smiling, felt its caresses, and tasted, too, its cups of bitterness and disappointment and sorrow. The little child knew nothing yet of life, its trials, dangers, pains, and losses. All that she knew was love and tender care. Yet there both of them knelt before the cross, and both of their faces, the seared and lined face of the aged man and the beautiful face of the little child, were transfigured by prayer. Yes, prayer transfigures the face. Anger, hate, envy, greed, passion always flee away before the beauty of prayer. When Stephen was praying, as they stoned him near the gate, his murderers saw his face "as it had been the face of an angel."

## THE MESSAGE OF MOSES AND ELIJAH

When Jesus prayed in Gethsemane, there appeared an angel to strengthen Him. But when He prayed here on the Mount of Transfiguration, there appeared not angels but two redeemed men, two of the greatest of the prophets, Moses and Elijah. The three chosen disciples had failed Jesus, but now, for His strength and comfort, God broke the seals of the world of the dead and brought forth Moses and Elijah to talk with Christ. Why these two? Although they were admittedly great, both of them, there were other great personalities of the Old Testament. Why not Abraham and Jacob? or Joseph and Joshua? or Gideon and Samuel? or David and Isaiah? or Jeremiah and Daniel?

There were good reasons for the divine selection. Both Moses and Elijah in their day, surrounded by danger and peril and threat and denied by the people whom they would deliver, had made their magnificent witness for God and had endured as "seeing him who is invisible." Perhaps above all others, they could testify to God's never-forsaking grace. Both could encourage Jesus to endure to the end. Both could testify that their labor had not been in vain in the Lord, though both had experienced hours when their labors did seem to amount to nothing—Moses on Nebo's lonely mountain, when he was forbidden to lead the people into the Promised Land; Elijah beneath the juniper tree in the desert, when he said, "It is enough; now, O Lord, take away my life; for I am not better than my fathers." Both of them, too, could testify to Jesus that God's way is always best. Moses could tell how he had prayed eagerly and vainly, as he thought, to be permitted to enter the Promised Land; but now, standing on the Mount of Transfiguration and conversing with Jesus, he would know that God's way is best and that God's answer was greater than he had desired. And Elijah could testify that if God had answered his prayer there beneath the juniper tree, he would not have made his sublime exit from earth and entry into heaven in a whirlwind, accompanied by a chariot and horses of fire.

CHRIST ON HIS DEATH

What did they talk about with Jesus on the mount? They talked with Him about the events that were not far distant— His decease, His death, His exodus which He should accomplish at Jerusalem. That was what the ages had waited for—the mighty act, conceived in infinite love, carried out by infinite power and approved by infinite justice, whereby guiltless blood for guilty man was shed and the price paid, the sublime, stupendous, overwhelming, awful price for man's redemption from sin and death. There were other great events in the history of redemption of the people of God about which they might have talked with Jesus. They might have talked with Him about the night of doom, when the angel of the Lord slew the firstborn of Egypt but passed over the blood-sprinkled homes of Israel. They might have talked with Him about the passage of the Red Sea, about Abraham offering up Isaac on the mountain, about the crossing of the Jordan; all that would have been appropriate and prophetically related to the coming event. But that grand history they passed over and talked only about His atonement, about His death, about the Cross.

There is the touchstone of New Testament faith. There is the dividing line among Christians; there is the secret of the difference in Christian thought and life. Does the man delight to speak of it? Or does he take it for granted and make no mention of it? Or does he say that it is too great to be explained and therefore ignore it? Moses and Elijah show the way. They give us the key to Christian conversation.

John could have talked there on the mount with Jesus and could have said, "The blood of Jesus Christ his Son cleanseth us from all sin." John the Baptist could have talked with Jesus there and said, "Behold the Lamb of God, which taketh away the sin of the world." Peter could have talked with Jesus on the mount on the same subject and said that we would not be redeemed "with corruptible things, as silver and gold . . . but with the precious blood of Christ, as of a lamb without blemish and without spot." Isaiah could have talked with Jesus and Moses and Elijah on the mount and said, "He was wounded for our transgressions, he was bruised for our iniquities." David could have talked with Him there on the mount and said, "Blessed is he whose transgression is forgiven, whose sin is covered." John Newton could have talked with Jesus there on the mount and said,

> I saw one hanging on a tree
> In blood and agony.

Sir John Bowring could have talked with Him there on the mount and said,

> In the cross of Christ I glory,
>   Towering o'er the wrecks of time;
> All the light of sacred story
>   Gathers round its head sublime.

Cowper could have talked with Him there on the mount and said,

> There is a fountain filled with blood
>   Drawn from Immanuel's veins;
> And sinners, plunged beneath that flood,
>   Lose all their guilty stains.

And Isaac Watts could have talked with Him there on the mount and said,

> See, from his head, his hands, his feet,
>   Sorrow and love flow mingled down:
> Did e'er such love and sorrow meet,
>   Or thorns compose so rich a crown?

And all the redeemed in heaven and all the holy angels could have talked there on the mount with Jesus and with Moses and Elijah, as they talked of His atonement, His decease at Jerusalem, and, singing their new song, the song of Moses and the Lamb, could have said,

> Worthy is the Lamb that was slain to receive power, and riches, and wisdom, and strength, and honor, and glory, and blessing.

Does it thrill your soul and kindle your mind to talk about the redeeming death of Christ? Do you like to hear that "old, old story" in the hymns and in art and in music and in the sermon and in the Bible? Are you ready to sing with a heart full of humility, repentance, and love, "unto him that loved us, and washed us from our sins in his own blood"?

One day early in the eighteenth century a German artist, Stenberg, walking through the marketplace of his home town, was attracted by the face of a dancing gypsy girl. He invited her to come to his studio and sit for him, and with her as a model he painted his "Dancing Gypsy Girl." The little girl was much taken with what she saw in the artist's studio and watched him with great interest as he worked on a painting of the Crucifixion. One day she said to Stenberg, "He must have been a very bad man to have been nailed to the cross like that." "No," the artist said, "He was a good man. The best man that ever lived. Indeed He died for all men." "Did He die for you?" asked the girl. That question set the artist thinking, for he had not yet given his heart to Christ. One day he chanced to go to a meeting of the Reformers, who opened the Scriptures to him, showed him the way of salvation, and brought him to Christ. Then he went back to finish his painting of the Crucifixion, working this time, not only with an artist's skill and technique, but with the love that comes out of a believing heart.

When the painting was finished, it was hung in the gallery at Düsseldorf. One day a young aristocratic German count, wandering through the studio, paused before Stenberg's "Crucifixion." The painting moved him greatly and also the words that were written under it, 'This I did for thee; what hast thou done for me?" That set the young count to thinking about what he could do for Christ. The result was the founding of that noble pietistic and missionary brotherhood, the Moravians, for the young count was none other than Nicholas Zinzendorf.

Let me repeat the question which the gypsy girl asked of the artist as she looked at his painting of Christ on the Cross, "Did He die for you?" If He did, do you love Him? If He did, what are you doing for Him?

# 6

## WITH A HARLOT

Jesus stooped down, and with his finger wrote on the ground (John 8:6).

Walking through the art galleries of Europe, you are fairly certain to see two paintings in almost every exhibit. One is of the martyr St. Sebastian bound to a tree, with his murderers shooting the arrows at him. The other is of the woman taken in adultery. The great masters have done their work well in reproducing the second of these moving and dramatic scenes, but none of them can compare with the master portrait painter of the New Testament, John.

At the end of a long debate with the Jews the day before, the crowd had dispersed, every man to his own home, but Jesus had gone to the Mount of Olives, where He spent the night in meditation and in prayer. If even the Son of God required those turnings aside for periods of contemplation and prayer in order that He might fulfill His great mission, how much more do you and I! As De Quincey puts it in *The Confessions of an English Opium Eater*, "No man will ever develop the possibilities that are in him who does not at least checker his soul with solitude."

> By all means use sometimes to be alone.
> Salute thyself; see what thy soul doth wear.[1]

---

1. George Herbert, "The Church Porch."

The next morning Jesus was teaching in the temple. That does not mean within the sacred and beautiful enclosure, for only the priests entered those hallowed precincts. It means that He was teaching in one of the porches or corridors which surrounded the great structure. About Him had gathered a considerable company of people. Suddenly the Preacher was interrupted by a commotion, angry voices, a muffled cry or sob, and loud commands, "Open up! Open up! Make way!" In a moment a number of the scribes and Pharisees appeared, dragging along with them a woman, her hair disheveled, her garments in disarray, fear and anger stamped upon her face. Bringing her to Jesus and pointing at her, they said, "Teacher, this woman was taken in adultery, in the very act. Moses in the law commanded us that such should be stoned. What have you to say about it?"

Why did they bring the woman alone? Where was the other transgressor? Where was the man, whose identity was as well-known to the scribes and Pharisees as was that of the woman? The world has moved very slowly toward a single standard of morality for men and women. In fact it is only since the first World War that in Great Britain a wife has been able to bring suit for divorce against her husband on the ground of adultery. These scribes and Pharisees were probably not greatly shocked at the sin of which this woman was guilty, for morals were at a low ebb. Moreover the ancient law of Moses which provided stoning for such an offense was rarely invoked, and the law itself, as recorded in Leviticus, provided that both the adulterer and the adulteress, the man and the woman, should be put to death. All that the scribes and Pharisees had in mind was to impale Jesus on the horns of a dilemma, to put Him in such a position that whatever answer He gave, His influence as a teacher would be destroyed. If, on the one hand, He said, "Yes; let her be stoned," then they could accuse Him to the Roman authorities, for the Romans had taken the power of capital punishment away from the Jews. Even when Pilate suggested to the scribes and Pharisees later on that they take Jesus and try Him themselves, they reminded him that it was not

---

2. The case of the stoning of Stephen, Acts 7:59, was an instance where the mob broke the Roman law.

lawful for them to put anyone to death.[2] If, on the other hand, He said, "No; let her go free," then they could accuse Him to the Sanhedrin of teaching things contrary to the law of Moses. Whatever His answer was, they were sure that He would be discredited as a teacher and as the alleged Messiah. But Jesus gave them an answer, a profound, powerful, deep, and over-whelming answer, which none of them had expected.

The first thing Jesus did was to stoop down and write on the ground with His finger. The impression one gets from reading John's narrative—the account of an eye witness of the scene—is that the act of Jesus in stooping down there in the presence of this woman and her accusers and all the bystanders was an expression of grief and modesty and that He was shocked at the gross and shameless way in which they had confronted Him with the woman taken in adultery. No doubt that is in His act, and the purity of Jesus never stands out in more appealing colors than in this scene.

The scribes and Pharisees waited for Jesus to answer, but He continued to write on the ground. This is one of the dramatic silences of the Bible. No one in the crowd said anything. None of the apostles uttered a word. The scribes and Pharisees said nothing. The woman said nothing except to break the silence now and then with a sob. And Jesus said nothing but kept writing on the ground. At length, supposing that He was confused and that they had Him cornered, the woman's accusers began again to press Jesus and with a note of exultation in their voices asked Him once more what He had to say on the subject. "What sayest thou?" Then, giving them a look which, I suppose, none of them forgot, even to his dying hour, Jesus said that they could stone her, but upon this condition: "He that is without sin among you, let him first cast a stone at her."

Having said that, Jesus stooped down and began to write again on the ground. Once more that dramatic silence. Not a word from the crowd. Not a word from the apostles. Not a word from Jesus. Not a word from the scribes and Pharisees. "He that is without sin among you, let him first cast a stone." In silence each one of the accusers looked at the other, expecting that he would break the silence and reach for the first stone. But each man was convicted in his own conscience and smitten by the thunderbolt that Jesus had launched against them. In the face of the woman there was mingled hope and dread—no doubt more dread than hope. It could not be possible, she must have been thinking to herself, that there was not one among these highly venerated leaders of the people who was not himself a sinner. The chances seemed all against her. Yet there must have been a look of hope, too, on the woman's face because of the way in which Jesus had spoken those words. "He that is without sin among you, let him first cast a stone."

At length, after a silence which must have seemed to the poor woman ages long, to her great relief she saw each of her accusers walk slowly away from the presence of Christ and away from her. They "went out one by one, beginning at the eldest, even unto the last: and Jesus was left alone, and the woman standing in the midst." Jesus had not seen the scribes and Pharisees file silently and guiltily out. But after a little, lifting up His eyes, He saw that they were gone and that He was left alone with the woman. Speaking now to her and looking into her face for the first time, He said to her, "Woman, where are those thine accusers? hath no man condemned thee?" The woman answered—and this is one of the answers of the Bible the tones of which I would give all the world to hear, for the music of a soul rescued and forgiven by Christ was in that answer—"No man, Lord." Jesus said to her what she must have already known without His saying it, "Neither do I condemn thee: go, and sin no more."

Although I heard my professor father preach on several occasions, there is just one sermon the subject matter of which I can recall, and that is the sermon in which he described this scene of John's gospel. The power of a sermon, however, lies not in the ability of the hearer to recall the text or the subject years afterward but in the spiritual and moral impression made at the time the sermon was preached. Ever since John wrote that Jesus stooped down and wrote on the ground, men have wondered and conjectured what it was that He wrote. Thousands upon thousands of sermons have been written about Jesus—His person, His words, His love, His death, His resurrection, His ascension, His coming again in glory—but here is the only sermon which Jesus Himself ever wrote. Since He wrote it in the sand on the porch of the temple, whatever it was that He wrote quickly disappeared. The characters and the letters of the words that He traced out with His finger were soon trampled underfoot by the people coming to and from the temple or were quickly scattered and blown hither and yon by the wind. They are gone forever. But there are some truths in this great interview which are, as it were, written down for us by the finger of Jesus Himself and can never be obliterated.

## CONSCIENCE

Whatever He wrote there on the sand and dust, you can be sure of this: He wrote first of all, for the instruction and condemnation of those malignant, hard-hearted, and pitiless scribes and Pharisees, the word "conscience," for John says that after Jesus had called for one who was without sin to cast the first stone at her, "being convicted by their own conscience, [they] went out one by one." When Jesus said that, He did not mean, of course, that only a sinless man can judge or pass sentence upon another. If that were so, we would have to adjourn all our courts of justice, empty all our jails and prisons, and give the world back to anarchy, for there are no sinless judges or officers of the law. Neither did Jesus mean that every one of those scribes and Pharisees was himself guilty of adultery. By no means. Probably there were many reputable men among them.

Christ's meaning was this: "He that knows himself in his nature to be altogether free from sin, let him judge this woman and put her to death." If there was a man among them who was sure that he had no taint of sin at all upon his soul, then he might cast the first stone. The words of Jesus were a shock which awakened within them all a sense of sin and made them ashamed—cowards in His presence. They had come to hear Jesus condemn a poor woman; instead of that, they heard their own hearts condemning them. They had come to hear pronounced again the stern law of Moses; instead of that, they heard the still small voice of God speaking in their own hearts.

One of the old manuscripts of the Gospel has this interesting and striking addendum to the text of John 8:6 as we have it in our Bible. It reads, "Jesus stooped down, and with His finger wrote on the ground the *sin of each one of them*." If that is so, then as the scribes and Pharisees looked over the shoulder of Jesus, the face of each man must have blanched at one of the words—"profane swearer," "dishonorer of parents," "extortioner," "bribe taker," "wife beater," "thief," "liar," "adulterer." No wonder, then, that each man, convicted in his own conscience, turned and with lowered countenance walked silently out. However true to the original text that sentence, "and wrote on the ground the sin of each one of them," may be, it is true at least to the spirit of this interview, for nothing is plainer than that each man felt his own sin. Christ wrote out each man's guilt and then let each man condemn himself.

Here we have the sublime display of the power of Jesus to convict men of sin. These scribes and Pharisees were not all adulterers—probably none of them were—but in the searching presence of Jesus each felt himself a sinner. In the old legend of the Holy Grail, whenever a man came into the presence of the sacred vessel containing the blood which Jesus had shed on the cross for man's redemption, he felt the wound of long-forgotten transgressions begin to burn again within his soul. Yes; it is the presence of Christ which condemns us all and yet gives hope to us all and enables us to cry out, "God be merciful to me a sinner!"

## PITY

I am sure that there was another word that Christ wrote in the dust that day—"pity," or "compassion." There were two aspects in Jesus—two strains of speech and conduct. In one respect He was very severe. He made the way of eternal life hard. He said, "He that loveth father or mother more than me, is not worthy of me." He said, "If any man will come after me, let him deny himself, and take up his cross, and follow me." He said stern words about marriage and divorce. He said that the way to heaven is narrow and the gate strait, and few there be that find it. He spoke in great severity, too, to those who were severe in their judgment upon others, and with burning, scorching words, He denounced the scribes and the Pharisees. The other aspect of Jesus was His tenderness and compassion.

To the transgressor himself He was full of pity. We see that in His dealings with the publican Zacchaeus. We see it in His beautiful words to the woman who was a sinner and who washed His feet with her tears and dried them with the hair of her head. We see it again in His interest in the salvation of the much-married woman of Samaria. But preeminently we see that pity and compassion for the transgressor in His attitude toward this woman of John's story. He protected her from the harsh judgments of her accusers and from the cruel punishment which they wished to execute upon her. Thus He showed us how to deal with transgression. That was the spirit that Paul recommended to us when he said, "Bear ye one another's burdens," and again, "If a man be overtaken in a fault, ye which are spiritual restore such an one . . . considering thyself, lest thou also be tempted."

In George Eliot's novel *The Mill on the Floss*, when Maggie Tuliver was reproached by her brother Tom for what seemed to him wayward and dangerous conduct, Maggie reminded him how he had always enjoyed punishing her, even when she was a little girl who had always loved him better than anyone else in the world; how he would let her go crying to bed without forgiving her. "You have no pity," she said: "you have no sense of your own imperfection and your own sins. It is a sin to be hard; it is not fitting for a mortal—for a Christian." Yes; that is true. It is a sin to be hard; for a mortal, subject to temptation, it is not fitting, and above all it is wrong for a Christian, whose hope for eternal life depends upon the forgiving love of God in Christ.

In his "Universal Prayer," Alexander Pope asks humbly,

> That mercy I to others show,
> That mercy show to me.

The prayer is faulty, in the sense that if God's forgiveness were to be measured by ours, then woe to us. But it is correct and in harmony with the teaching of Jesus in so far as it emphasizes the truth that those who receive forgiveness from God ought themselves to show pity and freely from the heart forgive one another.

Then gently scan your brother man,
    Still gentler sister woman;
Tho' they may gang a kennin' wrang,
    To step aside is human:

Then at the balance let's be mute,
    We never can adjust it;
What's done we partly may compute,
    But know not what's resisted.[3]

## FORGIVENESS

Would that I had seen His face as He was writing there on the ground and again as He said to the woman, "Where are those thine accusers? hath no man condemned thee?" for the light in the face of Jesus is never so bright and glorious as when He confronts a penitent sinner. The scribes and Pharisees dared not condemn her, and Jesus would not condemn her. There was no condoning of her sin, and when the woman had been assured that she was free from condemnation and Jesus had told her to go and sin no more, I am sure she knew herself to be a sinner in a far different way than she had under the accusation of the scribes and Pharisees.

If Christ dismissed her and forgave her sins, we can be sure, too, that she was repentant. God loves to bestow forgiveness upon the penitent soul. The angels rejoice when they hear the word "repent" upon the lips of a returning sinner, and although the angels are not mentioned here, I think I can hear the music of their rejoicing. "There is, therefore, now no condemnation to them which are in Christ Jesus." Christ had not yet died for sinners upon the cross, yet the forgiveness which was granted unto this woman was the forgiveness of the Cross, for Christ is the Lamb of God slain from the foundation of the world. Who can measure the length and the breadth and the depth and the height of the forgiving love of God in Christ? If such a thing were possible, it would seem that the Holy Spirit almost exhausts the treasures of inspiration in describing the reach of the forgiving love of God: "I will remember their sin no more."

3. Robert Burns, "Address to the Unco Guid."

"Though ye have lien among the pots, yet shall ye be as the wings of a dove covered with silver, and her feathers with yellow gold." "Though your sins be as scarlet, they shall be as white as snow; though they be red like crimson, they shall be as wool." "As far as the east is from the west, so far hath he removed our transgressions from us." A minister once asked a converted engineer and scholar, who had been redeemed by the grace of Christ, to give him a calculation on that sum, to measure how far the east is distant from the west. The man took his pencil and began to calculate and then said, "It is impossible!" No; there is no measuring the immeasurable love of God.

HOPE

The last word that He wrote here in the dust was "Hope." That is the word without which man cannot live. What did He say to this woman? "Go, and sin no more." It was a word of warning; but more that that, I am sure, it was a word of hope. The woman would be going back to her old neighborhood, to her old acquaintances, with the stigma of widely known and widely published sin upon her. People would know now that she had been a woman of "easy virtue." It would be hard, and yet Jesus dismissed her with that word of hope, "Go, and sin no more!" I wonder if, when the redeemed souls enter heaven, they will be greeted by the angels who shall speak some word of encouragement and congratulation to those who enter the realms of the blessed? Yes; I think that may be true. There will be one angel who shall say to them as they pass, "Enter, and labor no more." Another shall say to them, "Enter, and suffer no more." Another shall say to them, "Enter, and groan no more." Another shall say to them, "Enter, and weep no more." Another shall say to them, "Enter, and fear no more." But beyond all other salutations in the power of its joy and its peace will be the salutation of that angel who shall say to the redeemed souls as they pass in through the gates into the city, "Go, and sin no more!"

# 7

## WITH A DEMONIAC BOY AND HIS FATHER

*Come out of him, and enter no more into him (Mark 9:25).*

The Bible is a book of tremendous contrasts. It begins with chaos—"the earth was without form, and void; and darkness was upon the face of the deep"; and then came the dawning of the light, the emergence of the firmament, the gathering together of the waters, and the gathering together of the seas. There is the contrast between moral, devout men like Enoch, who walked with God, and other men so corrupt and full of iniquity that it repented God that He had made man. There is tremendous contrast, too, in personalities: Jacob and Esau, Joshua and Achan, Samuel and Saul, Elijah and Jezebel, Jesus and Herod, John and Judas, Nero and St. Paul; and in the Apocalypse the Lamb of God on His throne and the beast out of the abyss, the New Jerusalem coming down from God out of heaven and the lake of fire that burns forever and forever. But here is the most overwhelming contrast of all: the Mount of Transfiguration with its soft fleecy clouds and its bright lights; the transfigured face of the Son of Man; the voice that spoke out of the cloud; the visitors in glory from the realms of the dead, Moses and Elijah; the three wondering apostles, Peter and James and John—and then, not far from the mount in the plain below the taunting and disputing scribes, the downcast and dejected apostles, the heartbroken, anguish-stricken father, and the poor demoniac boy, gnashing his teeth, foaming and wallowing in his convulsions when the demon tore him, a terrible epitome of the misery and woe and sorrow and degradation of mankind.

Raphael's last painting and, some think, his greatest, "The Transfiguration," which hangs in the Vatican gallery, is an attempt to depict that contrast. Floating in the heavens above is the form of the Savior, with Moses on His left and Elijah on His right. On the level below are the three disciples, Peter, James, and John, just rousing themselves out of their slumber and shielding their eyes with their hands from the effulgence of the glory of the transfigured Christ. In the third level, on the plain below, is the poor demoniac boy with his mouth wide open in his ravings, at his side his distracted father, and around them the rest of the disciples, some of whom are pointing upward toward Christ transfigured in the cloud, as if to express the idea that He alone can help this father and his afflicted son.

After the great experiences on the mount, where Jesus had found comfort and encouragement in the conversation He had with Moses and Elijah and in the confirming voice of the Father that had spoken out of the cloud, Jesus and the disciples came back to the plain below. Peter had wanted to stay there and build three tabernacles, so that they might retain the two heavenly visitors and Jesus in His glory. But mountaintops, both literal ones and those of spiritual experience, are not meant as abiding places. They are for our inspiration and encouragement in the work of life. So Jesus came back to the plain to take up the hard, rough journey that at length would lead Him into the shadows of Gethsemane and into the sixth-to-the-ninth-hour darkness of Calvary.

As soon as the people down on the plain saw Him coming with His disciples, they ran to greet Him, and, Mark says, they were "greatly amazed." We wonder why that was. Why should they be amazed? Certainly they did not expect Him to remain on the lonely mountain, and certainly they did expect that He would return again to His disciples. Who knows? Perhaps the countenance of Jesus held some lingering radiance of the glory of the Transfiguration, like the face of Moses when He came down from His interview with God "and wist not that the skin of his face shone."

When Jesus appeared in their midst, the disciples were engaged in some angry dispute with the scribes. Jesus said to the scribes, "What is it you are arguing about with my disciples?" Neither group seems to have answered this question, but it must have been plain from the haughty and triumphant looks of the scribes and the somewhat downcast countenances of the disciples that the scribes had got the better of the argument. What were they arguing about? It may have been some theory as to the best way to exorcise the evil spirits, or whether it could or could not be done. And while they were arguing the matter, the poor boy who had occasioned the dispute lay unhelped and unattended on the ground.

Since neither the scribes nor the disciples could or would answer the question of Jesus, the father of the boy said, "Master, I have wrought unto thee my son, which hath a dumb spirit." Encouraged by Jesus to describe the symptoms, the father went on and told how his son foamed and gnashed with his teeth and pined away and how he had brought him first to the disciples and asked them to cast out the demon, but they could not. When Jesus heard that He gave a sigh and exclaimed, "O faithless generation, how long shall I be with you? how long shall I suffer you?" The rebuke of Jesus for the lack of faith embraced all who were present—the scribes, the father, and especially His own disciples who had failed to cure the boy.

Then turning to the father, Jesus said, "Bring him unto me." Those who were holding the boy now brought him up to where Jesus was standing. He was a sad and terrible spectacle, for as they brought him one of his convulsions seized him and he fell on the ground and wallowed foaming, like a wild animal. In tender compassion Jesus said to the father, "How long has he been this way? Is it a recent ailment or one of long standing?" The father answered, "Of a child"—in other words, "Since he was born." There you have the complete, dark, mystery of iniquity. The boy's own life and seemingly that of his parents had had nothing to do with this terrible plight. He was like the blind man of whom Jesus said, "Neither hath this man sinned, nor his parents: but that the work of God should be made manifest in him." And truly here in this sad and pathetic and terrible case of human woe and suffering the glory of God was about to be manifested.

## THE CONFESSION OF FAITH

Encouraged still further by Jesus, the father went on to tell how sometimes when he was in one of these convulsions the boy would throw himself into the fire or into the waters. "But," he added, in one of the most eager and agonizing pleas ever made to Jesus, "If thou canst do any thing, have compassion on us, and help us!" Jesus said to him, "If thou canst believe"—almost echoing the father's own words—"all things are possible to him that believeth." It was as if He had said, "I can heal your child, and if you will believe, I *will* heal him." At that the father of the boy cried out, completely broken down now, his eyes streaming with tears, "Lord, I believe; help thou mine unbelief!"

What that father said showed a condition that is common to the heart of man, with faith and unbelief coexisting there. When we think of the great things of life, of our duty and our destiny and our salvation, both the voice of faith and the voice of doubt will speak. It was so at the beginning. God gave His word to the man and woman in the Garden, but the Tempter came to sow the seed of doubt and craftily said to the woman, "*Hath* God said?" When Jesus appeared on a mountain in Galilee after His resurrection, Matthew tells us that the disciples worshiped Him, "but some doubted." So faith and unbelief grapple with one another in the soul of man. But what was true of this heartbroken father when he said to Jesus "Lord, I believe; help thou mine unbelief," is true of all of us; we have the power and the will to choose the side of faith as against the side of unbelief. And when we make that choice, we can count on the help and the sympathy of God. This father, troubled no doubt and somewhat mystified by what Jesus had said to him and yet putting his trust in Jesus, resolved to be guided by his belief rather than his unbelief. He confessed his faith, and whatever doubt was left in him he asked Christ to over-come.

During this interview the people had gathered together, running from every side, to see if Jesus could succeed where His disciples had failed. Strong hands set the afflicted boy upon his feet again. Looking upon him, Jesus said to the demon that was in him, "Thou dumb and deaf spirit, I charge thee, come out of him, and enter no more into him." The thrill of that is particularly in the last part of what Jesus said, "*and enter no more into him.*" The father would be remembering many occasions when he had seen his boy free from the terrible convulsions and had begun to hope the child was permanently cured, only to see another and more terrible convulsion seize him. But now Christ relieved his mind. He said not only, "Come out of him," but also, "Enter no more into him."

There you behold all the power and majesty of the saving grace of Christ. When he dismissed the woman taken in adultery, he said to her, "Go, and sin no more," and that, I think, was not so much a warning as it was a word of comfort and assurance, letting her know that in the midst of her temptations she would have strength and grace now to overcome them. "Go, and sin no more!" That was what He said, too, to the woman who was a sinner and who had washed His feet with her affectionate and grateful tears and dried them with the tresses of her beautiful and abundant hair: "Your faith has saved you. Go in peace. You are now beyond the power of your tempters and your temptations."

THE MIRACLE

The evil spirit that was in the boy made use of his last opportunity to attack him and gave him one more fearful visitation before he left. The boy fell prostrate on the ground, the foam still on his mouth, the mouth still open, the eyes still fixed and staring. There was not a sign of movement, not a sign of life. Silently the people in the crowd, pressing around, looked over the shoulders of Jesus and the anxious father and saw the boy lying there, stretched motionless on the ground. The multitude was awed. No one had a word to say. At length one whispered to the person next to him, "He has cured him, but he has killed him! That boy is dead!" And the others looked wonderingly down on the boy and at length, speaking openly now, exclaimed, "The boy is dead! He has cured him, but He has killed him!" Then a scribe, recovering his old boldness and arrogance, remarked to one of his fellows, "Yes; He has cured him, but He has killed him. What sort of a cure is that? We could have done that ourselves. We could have knocked the boy on the head and that would have been the end of it. What sort of a physician or prophet is this anyway?" I think I can see the face of the father as he looked at Jesus, stared down on the prostrate form and the expressionless face of his boy, and then turned back to Jesus; and I think I can hear him say, "Master, you have cast out the evil spirit, but I am afraid you have killed my boy. There is no life in him. And yet, Master, I would rather have him lying there motionless and dead than see him again torn and rent with one of those fearful convulsions."

But no! the boy was not dead. All the people might have been saying, "He is dead!" But Jesus took him by the hand and lifted him up and gave him back to his father, and, I hope, to his mother too.

He took him by the hand! When He healed the woman who was sick unto death with a fever, He took her by the hand. When He healed the blind man, He took him by the hand. When He cleansed the leper, He touched him with His hand. When He restored the daughter of Jairus to her father and mother, He took her by the hand. That was the way Jesus worked. His Gospel was the Gospel of the kind, encouraging, sympathizing hand. You can all preach the Gospel with your hand. You can do that in the church from Sabbath to Sabbath. Now and then you may encounter some cold or unfriendly or discourteous person who resents the proffered hand of welcome and of friendship, but not often. Here come those who are lonely. Give them the hand of friendship. Here come those who are doubting. Give them the hand of a good will that they cannot doubt. Here come those who but yesterday drank a cup of sorrow and affliction. Give them the hand of sympathy. Here come those who are bowing under an unseen

burden. Give them the hand of strength. Here come those
who are pursued by some dangerous temptation. Give them
the hand of deliverance. And here come those who are on the
verge of decision, at their tenth hour, at the turning point of
their life, just between the winning and the losing. Give them
the hand that shall draw them over to the side of God. Preach
the Gospel that Christ preached, the Gospel of the hand! When
you preach that sermon, you back up and reinforce and illumi-
nate and illustrate the sermon preached by the minister.

## THE POWER OF PRAYER

Afterward, when Jesus had gone apart with His disciples
into the house of some friend, they came to Him and asked
Him privately, "Why could not we cast him out?" Jesus answered, "This kind can come forth by nothing, but by prayer
and fasting." In a broader sense and deeper sense too, Jesus
had already given the cause of their failure when, after the
father of the boy had related how he had brought him first to
the disciples and they could not heal him, He exclaimed, "O
faithless generation!" The reason for the apostles' failure was a
lack of faith, and the lack of faith in turn was due to a lack of
prayer, for prayer creates faith. Jesus had come Himself from
the mountain of prayer and out of that strength was able to
heal the demoniac and cast out the evil spirit.

Why does the church, why does organized Christianity, not
have greater influence upon human society than it does? Why
does it not cast out more of the evil spirits of greed and war
and cruelty and vanity and licentiousness? Before attempting
to answer that, let me remind you that the Christian church
has cast many a demon out of this world. Why are the great
stone benches of the amphitheaters of the ancient world silent
and overgrown with grass, where once the thousands cheered
the bloody combat between beast and beast, man and beast,
and man and man? Why is it that you do not see unwanted
infants and crippled children exposed in the woods and along
the highways? Why is it that our places of worship are not
today temples of lust and licentiousness? Why is it that every
third man today is not the slave of another man, as he was

when paganism was in its flower? Why is it that the whole world is shocked at the terrible tale of how an American airman was beheaded by his Japanese captors? Such an event would have shocked no one nineteen hundred years ago. To ask these questions is to answer them. Yes; Christianity has cast demons out of mankind. The world is bad enough with the church. What would it be without it?

Nevertheless the question still haunts us. Why not greater conquests today? Why not greater influence upon the life and practice of the world? Enemies of the church can give easy answers, and the wish is father to the thought. But the reason, the real answer, is found here in the words of Jesus. The reason for failure is the lack of faith. Even Jesus Himself, the evangelists tell us, did not do many mighty works among the people of His own country, except to lay His hands upon a few of the sick, because of their unbelief. If that was true of outside unbelief, how much more will it be true of inside unbelief? Nothing more terrible can happen to the church than to lose its belief, its faith in the Gospel. That is what the hour calls for today! A great and sweeping and thrilling revival of faith in the power of the Gospel, that it is the power of God to salvation. "This kind can come forth by nothing but by prayer and fasting!" You might state it this way, "Nothing but by prayer and unworldliness." The church today is short on prayer and long on worldliness, and those who are holding conferences and seeking to get at the root and secret of the church's trouble need go no further than these plain words of Jesus to His disciples, "This kind can come forth by nothing but prayer and fasting."

Let us remember this, too, in our own battles and struggles for our souls and for the high influence of the Christian life. We all have the evil anti-Christ, anti-God spirits which attack us and take up their lodging place within our breasts. But they can be conquered. They can be driven out. There is a price to be paid, however, and that price is prayer and fasting—earnest waiting upon God, surrendering our wills to His will, and asking Him to give us the victory. And this is the victory that overcomes the world, that world of evil without and that world of evil that would make our hearts its home; "this is the victory. . . even our faith."

# 8

## WITH A PERSECUTOR
## AND BLASPHEMER

*Saul, Saul, why persecutest thou me?* (Acts 9:4).

It is the hour of noon. In the midday heat the ancient city of Damascus, surrounded by its massive and hoary walls, lies still and quiet. In the courtyards of the great caravansaries the camels and other beasts of burden are lying down, and near them their drivers too are taking their ease. The bazaars are closed, the merchants asleep, and the streets of the city deserted as the population takes its noontime rest. Even the great waterwheels which move majestically around, lifting the water from the rivers into the luxuriant gardens, have ceased to move. In the trees the birds are silent. Not a sound is heard in Damascus save the murmur of the waters of the river Abana laving the walls of the city and encircling it like a lover's arm.

To the southeast rises the snowcapped summit of Hermon. Along the highway from the south, from the direction of Jerusalem, comes a small caravan, the little asses in front, the soft-footed camels swaying from side to side after them. In the east caravans cease to travel at noon and seek rest at some convenient oasis. But this caravan breaks all the rules of the road. It presses on without rest or stopping, on toward its goal, the city of Damascus.

With the caravan, directing its journey, is a man driven by a fierce purpose. The pace of the camels and the donkeys is too slow for him, and he strides on ahead, his staff in his hand and a look of inexorable determination on his face. He is the chief of the Gestapo of the priests at Jerusalem. In a brief period he has made a record as a persecutor and informer such as the priests have never had before. Everywhere he has sought out and hauled into prison those who have professed themselves the followers of the crucified impostor, Jesus. Having heard that a company of them has gathered together in Damascus, this inquisitor and persecutor has set out for that city, armed with credentials from the high priest at Jerusalem. Upon his breast you can see the sealed placard which reads: "Be it known unto all persons that the bearer of this placard is hereby clothed with authority from the high priest to search out and arrest and bring for trial to Jerusalem all persons who depart from the Law of Moses and who follow after the impostor, Jesus."

The driver of the camels comes forward to speak to this leader of the caravan and says to him, "Sir, it is the custom for caravans to halt at the hour of noon, and for men and beasts to take rest and refreshment in the shadow of the trees." The leader turns upon him and with anger in his voice answers, "Yes; but not this caravan. This caravan will not rest at noon. This caravan will not halt until it has reached the end of its journey"; and pointing with his lifted staff toward Damascus, visible now on the horizon, he adds, "Yonder is the end of this journey!" There is Damascus, the goal of his march, and there wait his helpless prey.

But suddenly at noontime there is a blinding flash of light. This man, Saul of Tarsus, and all his companions with him, fall prostrate to the ground. Then they all hear but he alone understands a voice speaking in majesty and authority, "Saul! Saul! Why persecutest thou me?" The dazed and astonished man knows that he has been confronted by God and that the voice speaking to him is one of divine authority. Frightened and half dazed, he calls out, "Who art thou, Lord?" The voice answers, "I am Jesus whom thou persecutest: it is hard for thee to kick against the pricks." When he hears that, Saul answers, trembling and afraid, "Lord, what wilt thou have me to do?" The voice then tells him to go into the city, and there he will learn what God wants him to do. How different is Saul's entry into Damascus from what he had expected and planned. Instead of the proud and haughty persecutor looking fiercely about for his prey, saluted with honor by the leaders among the Jews of Damascus and looked upon with dread and horror by his proposed victims, we see a broken man, trembling, shocked, blind, helpless, led by the hand of others into the city. The shops and bazaars and houses are now beginning to open again as the people go about their work once more. From one of the houses where followers of Jesus live, a boy runs out to the caravan and asks who the man is that is being led blind into the city. He is told that it is Saul of Tarsus, chief of the Gestapo at Jerusalem. The boy runs back into the house to tell his father and mother. When the father hears that, he exclaims, "Saul of Tarsus! That cruel persecutor! God be praised! He hath confounded the devices of our enemies and delivered us out of the mouth of the lion."

Saul was taken to the house of a Jew named Judas on the street called Straight, an arched highway that ran and still runs straight through the city. In an upper room a mattress was unrolled for him on the floor, and there the trembling Saul lay down. For three days and three nights, taking no food and no water, he lay there, his sightless eyes staring out at the ceiling above him. Who can tell what Saul thought, felt, experienced, suffered, hoped, prayed during those three days and three nights? Echoing in his soul was that voice, "Why persecutest thou me?" As he lay on the floor there passed before him as in a vision all those whom he had persecuted and done to death because they believed in Jesus. He saw the mild old carpenter whom he had dragged out of his shop to his trial and death. He saw the young stonemason whom he had dragged from the embrace of his wife, and he heard again the cries of that wife and the babe in her arms. He saw once again the three fishermen from Galilee as he arrested them on their return from Jerusalem, half way down to Tiberias, and dragged them back to prison. But worst of all, he saw Stephen, kneeling in the bottom of the pit, the blood pouring from his wounds as the stones rained down upon him. And above the shouts and jeers of the mob he heard once more Stephen's final prayer, "Lord, lay not this sin to their charge." And through it all, echoing again and again, came those words, "Why persecutest thou me?"

At the end of the three days there came a vision to a Christian in Damascus by the name of Ananias; he heard God tell him to go over to the house of Judas and inquire for Saul of Tarsus. This man, he was told, had seen in a vision a man named Ananias coming to him and putting his hands on him and saying, "Receive thy sight." When Ananias heard that, he said, "Oh, no! Surely, Lord, you do not want me to go and talk to that man! Why, he is the man who has done so much evil to thy church and to thy followers in Jerusalem, and we had word that he was coming to Damascus to arrest and imprison everyone who calls on thy name." But the Lord said to Ananias, "Go thy way: for he is a chosen vessel unto me, to bear my name before the Gentiles, and kings, and the children of Israel: for I will show him how great things he must suffer for my name's sake."

With that, Ananias did as he was bidden. Entering into the house of Judas and seeing Saul, he put his hands on him and said, "Brother Saul, the Lord, even Jesus, that appeared unto thee in the way as thou camest, hath sent me, that thou mightest receive thy sight, and be filled with the Holy Ghost." Immediately Saul opened his eyes. Ananias then baptized him into the faith of Christ, "and straightway he preached Christ in the synagogues, that he is the Son of God."

If we are to judge by the results, this is the most momentous of all the interviews of Jesus. It resulted in the conversion of Saul of Tarsus, and that conversion of Saul is, after the Resurrection of Jesus Himself, perhaps the mightiest evidence of the truth of the Christian religion. This work of grace was effected by the appearance of Jesus to Saul. In his catalog of the resurrection appearances Saul lists it along with the others to Peter and James and the other apostles: "Last of all he was seen of me also, as of one born out of due time." With the change in Saul's heart and life the chief enemy of Jesus became Paul, His chief friend; the chief persecutor became the chief advocate. The man who had run through the world breathing out threats and slaughter against Christ and His church now commenced his incredible journeys throughout the world to find souls whom he could win for Christ and His kingdom. From this converted persecutor, Saul, blasphemer and bigot, came the greater portion of the New Testament, the sweetest lyrics of Christian love, the sublimest statements of Christian doctrine, and the noblest example of a Christian life.

## "BROTHER SAUL"

Saul was converted in an extraordinary way by the visible presence and glory of the risen Christ; yet we must not forget that in the conversion of Saul, in bringing him into the fullness of faith and into the fellowship of the church, Jesus made use of a humble disciple of his at Damascus. That man was Ananias. We never hear of him again, but his name is immortal because of the part he played in bringing Saul into the kingdom. It was an amazing triumph of Christian faith and Christian love for Ananias to go over to the house of Judas and talk to the bloody persecutor, Saul of Tarsus. He took him by the hand and called him "Brother," and when Saul opened his eyes, the first sight that he saw was the kind, Christian, forgiving face of Ananias.

In a dream I found myself in heavenly places where every sound was sweet music and every sight overwhelmed my soul with glory and grandeur. Looking about, I saw in one of the highest places of heaven one whom I recognized to be Peter, and near him, very close to him, another stood. I asked one of the angels who he might be and was told, "It is Peter's brother, Andrew, the man who brought him to Christ. That is why he has the seat of honor at the right hand of Peter." Then, in a yet higher place, the highest of all in heaven except that of the throne and the cherubim and the seraphim, I saw standing one whom I knew to be Paul, and at his right hand stood another. I asked the angel who was conducting me who that man was. Was it Timothy, whom Paul called "My dearly beloved son"? Was it Titus? Was it Onesimus, whom he redeemed from sin and slavery? Was it Onesiphorus, who had not been ashamed of Paul's chains at Rome and had often refreshed him? Was it Barnabas, who had vouched for Paul and started him on his

great work? Was it Silas, who accompanied him on his journeys? Was it Luke, his beloved physician? No! None of these
had that place of honor. It was Ananias, the man who took him
by the hand, the man who called him brother, the man who
brought him to Jesus!

## "WHY PERSECUTEST THOU ME?"

In the interview of Jesus with Saul there were three momentous questions. The first of these was asked by Jesus: "Saul,
Saul, why persecutest thou me?" Saul was amazed at that. He
thought that he had been persecuting only these deluded and
despicable people who had claimed that a criminal, crucified
on a cross, had arisen from the dead and was the Messiah of
Israel foretold by the prophets, who was to reign over the
earth. As for Jesus, He was nothing. He was in the grave where
they buried Him after His crucifixion. But now Saul learned
his mistake. Jesus was not in the grave. He was alive. He appeared to Saul and Saul heard His voice: "Why persecutest
thou me?"

In persecuting the disciples of Jesus, Saul had been persecuting Jesus Himself, the Lord of glory. Jesus identified Himself with His disciples. Two of the most celebrated names
among the martyrs were the two Wigtown martyrs, Margaret
Wilson, eighteen years of age, and Margaret MacLachlan, sixty-
three years of age. For their adherence to the doctrines of the
Covenanters during the "Killing Times" in the seventeenth
century they were sentenced to death by drowning in the waters of Bladnoch, where that river flows into Solway Firth.
The older woman was fastened farther from shore. Soon the
hungry remorseless tide was at her ankles, her knees, her waist,
her breast, and then up to her head. Thinking that the sight of
her struggles would change the mind of the younger Margaret
and make her recant, the persecutors pointed to the dying
Margaret MacLachlan and asked what she saw. "What do I
see?" said Margaret Wilson. "I see Christ suffering in one of
His members. Think that we are the sufferers? No. It is Christ
in us, for He sends none a warfare on their own charges."
Soon the hungry tide which had engulfed the older woman

swept over the younger, and another of those noble souls who "loved not their lives unto the death" had passed to her reward.

"I see Christ suffering in one of His members." It is well to remember that. Jesus identifies Himself with His faithful followers. Whoever hurts, wounds, wrongs, slanders a follower of Jesus is persecuting Jesus Himself. There are different ways of doing that. A Christian man who hurts or wrongs another Christian man is persecuting Christ. A Christian man who lives an unworthy life is persecuting Jesus. A man who assails the church of Christ or in the church does what is unworthy is persecuting the Son of God. A man who opposes Christ, who scorns and rejects His love, is persecuting Jesus, and to that person Jesus speaks as plainly and clearly as He spoke to Saul outside the gates of Damascus, "Why persecutest thou me?"

## "WHO ART THOU, LORD?"

Saul was conscious now of the presence of the Son of God. I think it was not merely a question but also an affirmation, as if Saul asked and then answered his own question, "Thou art Jesus, the Son of the living God."

That is the first and fundamental question of the Christian faith. "Who is Jesus?" There are those who claim that that question can wait. The main thing is to do the will of Jesus. His rank will take care of itself. But this is the question that cannot wait. That is what the people of Jerusalem wanted to know when Jesus rode into the city on the foal of an ass, amid the cheers of the multitude, "Who is this?" That is what the scribes and Pharisees wanted to know, "Who is this?" Do we not know His brothers and His sisters? Is he not the carpenter's son?" That is what Pilate wanted to know when Jesus stood in the judgment hall: "Art thou the King of the Jews?" And that is what Jesus Himself wanted to know of His disciples, "Whom say ye that I am?" When we have the faith and conviction that Jesus is the Son of God, Lord over all, then we have a rock upon which we can stand. Because He is the Son of God, His teaching is infallible and His words will endure forever; because He is the Son of God, He has the power through His death on the cross to forgive all our sins.

## "What Wilt Thou Have Me to Do?"

Immediately Saul saw that all he had been doing up to this time was a cruel and terrible mistake. All his tremendous energy and enthusiasm had gone in a wrong way and for a sinful cause. But Paul wasted no time mourning over the past. He knew at once that he was the chief of sinners, but he also knew that if Jesus, the Son of God, had appeared to him in that way and had changed him, that there was something that Jesus wanted him to do. "Lord, what wilt thou have me to do?"

Christ has a work for every follower of His to do. There is a work that you alone in your place can do for Christ. Never doubt that! What if everyone should earnestly and prayerfully ask Christ that question, "Lord, what wilt thou have me to do?" Oh, then what lives would be changed! What dispositions transformed! What chains of evil habit broken! What sins forsaken! What good deeds done!

Saul was the man who did not say No to God. But, you say, if God were to speak to me the way He spoke to Saul, if Christ were to appear to me and speak to me in a blinding flash of glory as He did to Saul of Tarsus at the gates of Damascus, then I would not find it hard to obey His voice and do His will. If you wait for an experience like Saul's, you will never be converted. You will never be saved. You will never do the will of God. Saul's conversion was not only for his good, but for your good and my good. He says that he was converted and obtained mercy that he might be an example and an encouragement for every man who is out of Christ, showing how willing God is to save and how He can save even to the uttermost. How amazing, how astonishing that the prince of glory, seated at the right hand of God, should have come down, should have condescended to appear to one man, and that one man His worst and His most cruel enemy upon earth! Amazing grace!

> Amazing grace! how sweet the sound,
>   That saved a wretch like me!
> I once was lost, but now am found,
>   Was blind, but now I see.

Saul did not say No to God. In spite of that overwhelming vision of the glory of God he could have said No. But he tells us that he was not disobedient to the heavenly vision. If God speaks to your heart, if it should please Him to use the story of this interview of Jesus with Saul, of the conversion of this great sinner to Christ, to touch your heart, to speak to you and say, "Why persecutest thou me?" then do not say No to God, but, like Saul, be obedient to that voice and to the light of that vision.

# 9

## WITH A MAN THEY COULD NOT HUSH

Whereas I was blind, now I see (John 9:25).

Thou art not yet fifty years old, and hast thou seen Abraham?"

This came at the end of a long debate Jesus had with the Pharisees. They wanted to know if He thought He was greater than Abraham their father. To this Jesus said, "Abraham rejoiced to see my day: and he saw it, and was glad." Angered and amazed, they said to Him, "Thou art not yet fifty years old, and hast thou seen Abraham?" Then came that great and impressive answer of Jesus, "Verily, verily, I say unto you, Before Abraham was, I am." At that they took up stones to stone Him. But Jesus hid Himself from them and, passing through the crowd, left the temple precincts.

As He was passing, He saw by the roadside a man who had been blind from his birth. To the disciples of Jesus this poor man was not a subject for healing mercy, but just a suggestion for a theological question and problem: the relationship of sin and suffering. That problem is as old as humanity, as old as suffering and sin. In this particular case the question was more acute than ever because the man had been born blind. The disciples said to Jesus, "Master, we believe, in common with all the teachers of our race and faith, that suffering and misfortune such as this are the result of sin and the punishment upon sin. But what about this man, this blind beggar here? He was born blind. Now tell us, who did sin, this man or his parents, that he was born blind?"

The disciples were wondering if his soul had sinned before he came into the world. There were groups among the Jews at that time who believed in the preexistence of souls and in the transmigration of souls. Evidently the idea had filtered through in some form to these unlearned fishermen who were the disciples of Jesus. If the man had not sinned before he was born, then, they wanted to know, had his parents sinned and was that the cause of his blindness? There is indeed a great deal of physical weakness and disease and, not infrequently, blindness that is the result of the transgression of parents before the afflicted one was born. God visits the iniquities of the fathers upon the children, even to the third and fourth generations. The innocent suffer because of the guilty. Every battlefield reverberates that truth; every hospital ward echoes it. It is a mystery which many a babe's helpless cry proclaims: the innocent suffers for the guilty.

Jesus answered, however, that there was no immediate connection between the blindness of this poor man and the transgression of his parents. "Neither," He said, "hath this man sinned, nor his parents: but that the works of God should be made manifest in him." Jesus dismissed the problem of evil and the speculation about the causes of the man's affliction with those words. God had permitted blindness to come upon him, but the end of that permission and the end of that affliction would be the manifestation of the glory and the power of God.

When we look at the world with all its woes and suffering and then think about God, we might feel that we are forced into one of two positions or convictions: One, that God is omnipotent and therefore not all good, since He permits evil. The other, that God is good and would like to prevent evil but cannot; therefore He is not omnipotent. But here Jesus gives us the Christian view, the Christian doctrine of evil and its solution, that God will bring good out of evil, that all things work together for good; and thus

We trust that somehow good
   Will be the final goal of ill,
To pangs of nature, sins of will,
   Defects of doubt, and taints of blood;

That nothing walks with aimless feet;
   That not one life shall be destroyed;
Or cast as rubbish to the void,
   When God hath made the pile complete;

That not a worm is cloven in vain;
   That not a moth with vain desire
Is shriveled in a fruitless fire,
   Or but subserves another's gain.[1]

## THE BLIND MAN WITH CHRIST

From the discussion of the problem of moral evil and physical evil, Jesus turned to minister to this blind man. In that, perhaps, there is a suggestion for us all. The thing to do when we see moral evil and physical pain is not to debate about it but do what we can to relieve it. A wise expositor of the Scriptures has written that as for these difficult problems, like the problem of evil as related to an omnipotent and infinitely good God, we shall be better equipped in eternity to discuss them than we are now and shall have much more leisure for that discussion.

Before proceeding to heal the blind man, Jesus said, "I must work the works of him that sent me, while it is day: the night cometh, when no man can work." He was thinking, of course, about the great day of opportunity and the day of His earthly ministry, which was rapidly drawing to a close. But the solar day, that very day in which He was speaking and living, was drawing to a close too, and the long shadows were beginning to fall across the Mount of Olives and the Holy City. Jesus said He must make haste and heal this man before the day was over and the night had come. If even Jesus in the days of His

---

1. Tennyson, *In Memoriam*, liv.

flesh subjected Himself in His work and ministry to the limitations of time, although He was the Lord of time and is the same yesterday, today, and forever, how much more must you and I act in view of that solemn limitation of time! For the work of life, for the work of repentance, for the work of ministry to our loved friends, the day is brief and the night comes when no man can work. How many, alas, have awakened too late to discover that the shadows are gathering about their path, that the night is coming down upon them, and that now the work that can be done only in the daytime will never be done. That great Scottish saint, Robert McCheyne, was wont to seal his letters with a sun going down on the mountain, a symbol of the shortness of the day that was granted him for doing God's will. On the face of the watch that he carried, Samuel Johnson had inscribed these words of Jesus, as they are written in the Greek Testament, *Ercetai nuvx*—"The night cometh." That is the way to think of life, not as so many years to be lived through, with its different ages and states—youth, middle life, and old age—but as an appointed period for the doing of God's will.

"The night cometh!" If there is any improvement that you want to make in your life, make it now. The night comes! If there is any good work that you would like to do, do it now. The night comes! If there is any word of appreciation or encouragement that you would like to speak, speak it now. The night comes! If there is any word of regret that you would like to speak, speak it now. The night comes! If there is any deed of amendment and restoration that you would like to do, do it now. The night comes! If there is any deed of affection that you would like to do for one whom you love, do it now. The night comes! If you have not yet repented, if you have not yet put your faith in Christ as your Savior, repent now; for the night comes, and after the night comes there is no repentance.

Before that day ended, before its light was spent and night had come down, Jesus did a great work of divine power and mercy. In nearly all the other miracles of which we have a record, He healed the afflicted in response to their cry for help. But here there had been no word of request from the blind man unless it had been a request for alms. Of His own initiative Jesus healed the man. First of all He anointed the man's eyes with clay, mixed with saliva, and then told him to go and wash in the pool of Siloam. He could have healed the man as He had healed many others, immediately by the word of His power, but, for His own reasons, and no doubt for the sake of the greater miracle that He was going to work, He healed this man gradually and gave him a part to play in the miracle.

How quick and complete was the man's obedience! He might have said, as he said later on, "Since the world began was it not heard that any man opened the eyes of one that was born blind." But instead of doubting or questioning, he immediately arose and with full faith in the words that the stranger had spoken to him started off for the pool of Siloam. You can see him feeling his way along the street, touching the wall and the pavement with his staff, moving down this street, around that corner, and past one building after another, and then going out through the gate in the direction of the vale of Hinnom until he reached the pool. Making his way through the loiterers who lay about it, he went down into the water and, putting both his hands into the pool, washed his eyes as Jesus had commanded him to do.

As soon as he had done that, he received his sight. That is just a historical record. As John put it, he "came seeing." But imagine what that meant to him! When I read how Jesus healed this blind man and Bartimaeus and the rest of them, I often wonder how they felt. How did the first look of this world, upon which you and I have looked from the day we were born, but upon which the man born blind had never looked—how did it strike him? That clear water of Siloam's pool, the forms of the men standing about the pool, the mountains in the distance, the blue dome of the sky, the temple, at the gate of which he had sat begging for so many years, and then the face of his father, his mother, his brother, his sister? How did it strike him? *All* that was wonderful to him. And yet the most wonderful thing he had not yet seen, and that was the face of the Man who had healed him.

## WITH THE NEIGHBORS

When he appeared at his home, he created a great sensation in his family and among the neighbors. They looked upon him with astonishment and yet with incredulity, and one said to another, "Is not this he who was blind, he whom we have seen sitting there begging for the last twenty years?" Some answered, "It certainly is he, he and no one else." But others could hardly believe their senses and said, "No, it is not he; but it is someone like him." But the man himself put an end to their debate by saying emphatically, "I am he. I am the man who was blind. Now my eyes are opened."

The neighbors said to him, "How in the world did it happen? Tell us how your eyes were opened." He answered, "A Man called Jesus stopped where I was sitting as He passed by, and, after saying something to His disciples about how He was the Light of the World and how He must work while it was still day, before the night came on, He anointed my eyes with clay and spittle and told me to go wash in the pool of Siloam. I went and washed and I received my sight."

"Who is it that could do this great deed?" they asked, "and where is He?" The man said, "I don't know; I never saw Him after He spoke to me and after I received my sight."

## WITH THE PHARISEES

The case was so unusual that the neighbors decided to bring the man to the Pharisees. Furthermore, it happened to be the Sabbath day when Jesus healed the man. The first interview had been between the man and his neighbors; the second interview was between the man and the Pharisees. They asked him what the others had asked, how he had received his sight, and he gave them the answer that he had already given to his neighbors. Some of the Pharisees who did not believe that he had been healed of blindness and others who believed but were not moved by the event remembered only that it was the Sabbath day when Jesus had healed him and said, "Well, this man is not of God because in curing a blind man on the Sabbath day, He has broken the Sabbath." But others of the

Pharisees, more sensible and more humane, said, "How could a man that is a sinner do such great miracles?" Then they appealed again to the blind man and said, "What have you to say about this man who healed you? What sort of man do you think He is?" The man replied, and it shows how his conviction and understanding about Jesus was growing, "He is a prophet!" That was the highest tribute that a Jew could pay to a living man. That was what the woman of Samaria said to Jesus after He had searched her heart and told her all the things that ever she had done: "Thou art a prophet." So this man gave his verdict about the One who had healed him: "He must be a prophet; He is a man of God and from God."

The Jews, still unwilling to believe that the man had really been blind and that Jesus had healed him, now summoned his father and mother, hoping that they would admit that the whole thing was a hoax. "Is this your son?" they said. "Yes, he is our son." "Was he born blind, as he said he was?" "Yes, he was born blind." "How then were his eyes opened?" "That," they said, "we don't know. He is of age. Ask him, he can speak for himself."

Dismissing the parents, the Pharisees summoned the man before them and began to badger him once more. They said to him, "Give God the praise: we know that this man is a sinner." They did not mean, "Praise God for the miracle of your healing," but, "Be honest with God now and confess that you were never healed; because we know that this man Jesus, whom you claim to have healed you, is a sinner." To this the man, not committing himself on the particular point that the Pharisees were pressing, namely, whether or not Jesus was a sinner, gave his answer, and a greater tribute to the power of Christ was never paid, "Whether he be a sinner or no, I know not: one thing I know, that, whereas I was blind, now I see."

Unwilling to be convinced, the Pharisees for the third time asked the man, "What did He do to you? How did He open your eyes?" To this new cross-examination the man answered, "I have told you already, and ye did not hear: wherefore would ye hear it again? will ye also be his disciples?" Generally that question has been considered ironical, but I think it was a simple and earnest and sincere question on the part of this

man who himself was resolved in his heart to be the disciple of
Jesus. He thought so much of Him that he would have even
these badgering Pharisees know Him and trust Him. But the
very mention of that enraged them. "We," they said, "become
disciples of this Man! We are the disciples of Moses. As for
this fellow, we know nothing about Him." Then the simple,
but powerful defender of Christ said to them, "That is a most
marvelous thing, that you, the religious leaders of the people,
know nothing of this Man who has opened my eyes and since
the world began it was not heard that any man opened the
eyes of one that was born blind." With that the Pharisees
brought the interview to a close by saying, "Are you trying to
teach us? To preach to us? You, who were altogether born in
sin?" And they cast him out, forbade him to come to the synagogue, excommunicated him.

## WITH CHRIST AGAIN

Now comes the dramatic and moving conclusion, the second interview of the man with Jesus. Someone told Jesus that
the man whom He had healed had been cast out. Jesus did not
say, "That is too bad. However, he has his eyesight, and that
will compensate him for being excommunicated." No; instead
of that He sought for the man and found him. Here is the
Good Shepherd seeking for the one sheep that was lost, and it
is important to remember that this passage in John about the
blind man really comes to an end in the tenth chapter with the
words of Jesus about the shepherd and the sheep.

When Jesus found him, perhaps somewhat cast down and
disconsolate and already, as was the custom with those who
had been excommunicated, shunned and ostracized and scorned
by the people as an unclean thing, Jesus said to him, "Dost
thou believe on the Son of God?" The man had never seen
Jesus up to this time, for he was still blind when Jesus told him
to go and wash in the pool of Siloam. But he surely remembered the voice; or, if he did not remember it, the voice now
stirred his soul to the depths, for, as Jesus Himself said, "My
sheep hear my voice." Looking upon Jesus, the man said, "Who
is he, Lord, that I might believe on him?" He felt that he had

been called to the highest, that a great opportunity was opening before him and, like a wise soul, he wanted to embrace it. "Who is he, Lord? Where is he, that I might believe on him?" Jesus said, "Thou hast both seen him, and it is he that talketh with thee." To that the man answered, "Lord, I believe!" "And he worshipped him." Faith leads to worship. This man believed in Jesus as the Son of God, and immediately he followed Him and worshiped Him.

Such is the great story of the passage of a soul from darkness into light. It is the story of a man passing from physical blindness into the wonderful light of this world. But far more than that, it is the story of a soul passing from spiritual darkness into spiritual light. When that happens, a man knows it. There can be no doubt about it. The main thing is not the way in which it happens, the different paths by which one comes to the light, the different experiences of conversion. The main thing is that you have come out of darkness into light, that you are standing now in the light, and that you can say, "One thing I know, that, whereas I was blind, now I see."

## WITH HIS FELLOWS

Men have different experiences in coming to the light, different ways in which their blindness is healed by Christ. Let us suppose that all those blind men whom Jesus had healed got together once and had a testimonial meeting. First the two from Jericho got up and related how they called on Him to have mercy on them, and Jesus stood still and called them to Him and asked them what they wanted, and they said, "Lord, that our eyes may be opened," and how He touched their eyes and immediately they received their sight. And then those two from Capernaum got up to tell their story, how when they heard He was in the house, they came to Him, and Jesus said to them, "Do you believe that I am able to do this?" and when they said, "Yes, Lord," He said, "According to your faith be it unto you," and He touched their eyes and they were opened. And then the man from Bethesaida got up to give his testimony. He told how some of his friends brought him to Jesus and asked Him to touch his eyes; how He took him by the hand, led him out of the town, and, when He had anointed his eyes, put His hands on them and asked him if he could see anything; how he said, "I see men as trees, walking"; and how Jesus put His hands on the man's eyes once again, and this time when he looked up he saw clearly. And then Bartimaeus got up and told his story: how he was sitting that morning by the gate when he heard the footsteps of the multitude and, learning that Jesus of Nazareth was passing by, called out loudly and repeatedly, in spite of the attempts of those about him to silence him, "Jesus, thou son of David, have mercy on me!" how Jesus stood still and bade them call him; how he ran to Him and to the sound of His voice, blind though he was; how Jesus said to him, "What wilt thou that I should do unto thee?" how he said, "Lord, that I might receive my sight"; and how Jesus said to him, "Go thy way; thy faith hath made thee whole." And then this man born blind, the most wonderful cure of all, got up and told his story. All seven of them had different experiences, different ways in which Christ had opened their eyes; but every one of them, when he finished his testimony, was able to say, "Whereas I was blind, now I see!"

Can you say that too? Do you behold Christ as your Savior? Do you see Him as the one who by His precious blood washed away all your sins? If you do, then, as this man whose eyes were opened said to those who were questioning and doubting him, "Will ye also be his disciples?" so you can say to others:

> Come to the light, 'tis shining for thee,
>> Sweetly the light has dawned upon me,
>> Once I was blind, but now I can see,
>> The light of the world is Jesus.

# 10

## WITH A STREETWALKER

*And kissed his feet (Luke 7:38).*

Lights began to glow in the mansion of Simon the Pharisee. The servants were bustling to and fro in kitchen and pantry and dining hall, for Simon was giving a great supper on this night. Through the streets of the town men could be seen making their way toward Simon's house. In front of them walked servants holding torches in their hands to light the way for their masters. Outside the entrance to the house of Simon a group of the common people of the town had gathered to watch the notables arrive. As each passed by on his way to the door, the people made comment, sometimes favorable, sometimes unfavorable. First to come was Benjamin, the chief rabbi of a neighboring town, and after him Dives, the richest man in Capernaum. When he passed there was a half-subdued murmur of scorn, for the people did not like Dives. Then came Saul, a notable instructor in the Hebrew law, to whom the people gave the deference that the world has always paid to the scholar. So the guests assembled for the banquet to which they had been bidden.

Near the entrance there sat on one side two blind men, and on the other an impotent man, who, when they heard the footsteps of the approaching guests, put up their plaintive wail, "Have mercy on us!" and stretched out suppliant hands for the alms which were tossed to them. As the guests entered the atrium of Simon's house, a servant stationed there motioned each one to a stool and, when the guest had seated himself, brought a basin and towel, removed his sandals, and laid them aside and washed his feet. The guests then in bare feet proceeded to the banqueting hall. On the way another servant stopped them and from a vessel in his hand touched their heads with sweet-smelling oil. At the doorway of the hall stood Simon, handsomely arrayed in the blue and white robes of his office, with one phylactery bound to his left arm and another to his brow. As each guest approached him, Simon stepped forward and kissed him on the cheek and then motioned him to his place at the banqueting table. The table was not spread, as with us, in the middle of the room, but against the back wall, with the two ends extending a little in the shape of an L. Immediately back of this long table were the couches, backless couches strewn with tapestries and pillows upon which the guests reclined at ease as they reached for the things on the table which pleased their fancy. Between the couches and the wall was a space sufficient for the servants who waited on the table to pass up and down. The table was lighted with candles and with silver lanterns which hung from the ceiling of the room. In a courtyard on one side, half open to the dining hall, there was a fountain, and the guests could hear the soft murmur of its waters chant a pleasant antiphony to their own conversation.

The last guest to arrive was none other than Jesus Himself. Just why Simon invited Jesus is not quite clear. Perhaps he wanted to question Him on His attitude toward some portion of the Mosaic law or the Hebrew traditions. Perhaps it was just a matter of curiosity to see at close range one whose fame was beginning to spread through the land. Perhaps it was that common motive back of a good many invitations, to warm oneself in the limelight of a notable person. But whatever the motive, Jesus accepted the invitation. He accepted invitations to the houses of publicans and sinners, and, at the other extreme of Hebrew society, He accepted the invitation to the house of Simon.

THE DISCOURTESY OF SIMON

At a frown from Simon, the servant at the first entrance did not ask Jesus to be seated so that he might wash His feet in the basin. The other servant also let Him pass without anointing His head with oil, and Simon himself omitted the customary kiss of salutation and merely proffered his hand and waved Jesus to His seat. There was a good deal of lifting of eyebrows and whispering of comments when the other guests saw Jesus seated in their midst, for they remembered some of the things He was reported to have said about the Pharisees and the rich; how He had said it would be harder for a rich man to enter into the kingdom of heaven than for a camel to pass through the eye of a needle.

When all were seated Simon took his place, the seat of the host, not at the middle of the table but at one of the ends where he could survey all the guests. Then the servants brought in the huge bowls in which floated the savory meat which had been prepared for the banquet, and into these dishes each guest put his hand and took a generous sop. Occasionally a hungry scavenger dog came furtively under the table and was tossed a morsel by one of the diners. Now the wine was beginning to flow, and everyone, warmed with food and wine and cheered with the luxury of Simon's home, joined in the conversation, the murmur of which those waiting and watching without could distinctly hear.

## THE DECISION OF THE WOMAN

Outside, apart from all others, stood two lepers, looking with eager and wistful eyes at the scene of plenty and good cheer. Closer to the house stood another group of townsfolk, watching the banquet and the servants as they passed around the food. In a place by herself stood a solitary woman, evidently in the prime of young womanhood. When the soft evening wind lifted for a little the veil upon her head, it disclosed a face of unusual charm and beauty and yet great sadness, for beauty and sadness are closely related in life. Under her left arm and next to her heart she clasped a blue alabaster vessel, the kind that was used for precious and costly ointment. For a time the unknown woman, unobserved by the other loiterers, watched the scene of the banquet. Now lifting her skirt a little with her right hand, she moved forward toward the entrance to Simon's house. As she was stepping quickly and with wonderful grace toward the threshold, a hand was laid on her shoulder, and a Roman voice exclaimed, "Mary, is it you!" At that the woman quickly turned her head. The light shining out from the banqueting hall illuminated for a moment her beautiful face, and in her dark, lustrous eyes there was a look of recognition, half apprehension, half pleasure, as she gazed into the face of the man who had accosted her.

The man was Olynthus, officer of the Ninth Roman Legion. It was evidently the meeting of old friends. With eager, affectionate voice, drawing the woman aside a little, Olynthus said, "Mary, I have found you at last! Since that memorable evening beneath the stars at Cesarea with the sound of the waves of the sea breaking upon the shore, I have sought you long and carefully. Wherever our legion was encamped I looked for you—at Jerusalem, at Jericho, at the baths of the Dead Sea, at Tiberias, at Samaria, and in all the towns of Galilee—and yet I could never find a trace of you. Now, may Jupiter be praised, here you are—here in this town near which my legion is encamped, for we are on our way to put down an uprising in the territory of the Gadarenes. Jupiter and all the gods be praised! In six months, Mary, my furlough comes, and then back to Italy it will be for us, and I will show you all the wonders of that Roman world, all the sights and splendors and chariot races and gladiatorial battles of Rome, great Caesar's palace, the forum, and then my villa at Puteoli. Within three weeks we march through this town again. Be ready then, Mary, for our departure."

But to the surprise of Olynthus, Mary expressed no purpose to go with him. Though she had had many lovers, this was the only one who had really touched her heart, and for a moment the eager, affectionate voice of Olynthus had awakened an answering throb of affection in her own heart. But it was only for a moment. Laying a soft hand on his arm, she said, "Olynthus, you have always been kind and generous to me, and if I had known you sooner, life might have been different for me. Yet I do not complain at the ways of providence, for had my life been different, I could not now have within my heart the love that I now feel for another."

"Another!" exclaimed Olynthus. "And who is he?"

"Have no fear, Olynthus, He is my Lover, but also the Lover of all souls. He is the Eternal Lover, the peasant Prophet of Galilee."

"What!" said Olynthus, "that wandering, mendicant teacher of whom I have heard so much on my marches through the country! That man who goes about with twelve poor fishermen and peasants and even a despised publican and tax gatherer? Surely you will not forsake me for such a man as that!"

"Yes, Olynthus. Yet I do not forsake you, for this One has taught me to love all men. But now I must hasten, for here in this alabaster box I have precious ointment. Now must I hasten, or the banquet be over before I can kneel to anoint His feet."

With that she started again toward the doorway. Olynthus reached out a gentle but restraining hand, saying, "Mary, I cannot let you go! Think again before you leave me, before we part, for it may be forever."

Freeing herself from his grasp, the woman answered, "No, Olynthus. Let me go! The Eternal Lover is waiting for me." And with that Olynthus let her pass.

THE HOMAGE OF THE WOMAN

Entering the banqueting hall, for dinners and suppers then were far more accessible to the public than those held today, she passed softly and quietly to the place where Jesus reclined at the table and, standing behind Him, began to weep. At once the hum of conversation ceased as Simon and his guests stared at the woman. Their astonishment, however, was mingled with admiration, for in the full light of the candles and the candelabra and hanging lanterns everyone could see that the woman was beautiful in person and lovely of countenance. And yet they all knew that she must be a sinner, for no woman of reputation would appear in public alone at a banqueting table.

As she stood for a moment, the woman received from Jesus a look that gave her courage and hope. Putting aside the costly vase in which she carried the ointment, she knelt behind Jesus and, a flood of tears pouring from her eyes, fell upon His feet, unwashed because of Simon's incivility. She had brought no towel with her but washed His feet, those feet so soon to be pierced with nails upon the cruel cross, with her soft and shapely hands. Then laying hold on the tresses of luxuriant hair that fell over her shoulders and using them for a towel, she dried His feet. After that she broke the seal on the alabaster box and poured the ointment, not on His neglected head, but upon His feet, and the whole house was filled with the sweet odor of the ointment; the world ever since has been filled with that sweet odor. All the guests of Simon, without a word, were looking on. The lepers and the townspeople, standing apart, were watching in wonder, and they too were silent. And yonder in heaven, looking over its golden balustrades, even the angels looked down in heavenly wonder and delight.

During this remarkable scene, Simon had been thinking and saying to himself, "This Man, if He were a prophet, would have known who and what manner of woman this is that is touching Him, for she is a sinner; no prophet would ever let a woman who was a sinner touch him. This is one of the reasons why I invited Him to my banquet tonight. I wanted to scrutinize Him and see whether or not He is really a prophet. Now I know. He is no prophet. He is an impostor."

Strange, very strange how Jesus had changed the credentials of a prophet! When He talked with another woman who was a sinner, that woman of Samaria at Jacob's well, His disciples marveled that He would talk with such a woman. Here Simon and all his guests were certain that Jesus was no prophet because He let a woman who was a sinner touch even His feet. But today we hail Him as Prophet, we hail Him as the Son of God, because He received sinful men and women and touched them and let them touch Him.

All the time Jesus knew what Simon was thinking. Very arresting and solemnizing, sometimes frightening and condemning, at other times cheering and uplifting is that recollection that Jesus knows what we are thinking at every moment. Yes; He knew, as John wrote of Him long ago, what was in man. He knows our hearts today. O Lord, You who searches the heart and tries the reins, to whom all hearts are open and from whom no secrets are hid; by Your divine grace may I admit to the chambers of my heart only those thoughts and desires which I would like to have my Savior know.

## FORGIVENESS AND LOVE

Turning to His host, Jesus said, "Simon, I have somewhat to say unto thee." And Simon answered, somewhat brusquely no doubt, for he was a man accustomed to authority, "All right, Master, say on. Speak whatever is in Your mind. I shall be glad to hear it. I am sure my guests will not object."

Then Jesus told His brief parable, like Hamlet's play within the play. It was the story of a certain man who had two debtors. One owed him five hundred pence and the other fifty. Neither one had anything to pay the debt, and according to the hard custom of the day the creditor could have cast them both into prison. But instead of doing that, he freely forgave them. "Tell me, therefore, which of them will love him most?" Simon answered, "I suppose that he to whom he forgave most." His use of the word "suppose" here must have had an accent of indifference, but perhaps a little also of perplexity as to what the drift of the parable might be. Just what was Jesus getting at? Was He going to trap him with that question about the two debtors? Was He going to humiliate him before his guests? Yet there could only be one answer to the question, and Simon gave that answer, "He to whom he forgave most."

Jesus, lifting His voice said, "Thou hast rightly judged." Then, half turning to the woman who now had risen from her knees and stood behind Him, but addressing Himself to Simon, Jesus said, "Seest thou this woman? I entered into thine house, thou gavest me no water for my feet: she hath washed my feet with tears, and wiped them with the hairs of her head. Thou gavest me no kiss: but this woman, since the time I came in, hath not ceased to kiss my feet. My head with oil thou didst not anoint: but this woman hath anointed my feet with ointment. Wherefore, I say unto thee, Her sins, which are many, are forgiven; for she loved much: but to whom little is forgiven, the same loveth little."

Jesus did not say there, of course, that the woman was forgiven because she had loved much, but back of that, that she loved much because she had been forgiven much. Hers was the great debt, the five-hundred-pence debt, the debt of a woman who was a sinner; Christ had forgiven her, and now she loved much. Something that Simon, proud-hearted and self-righteous character, and none of his guests could understand or feel or appreciate was in this woman's heart—that greatest, deepest, most beautiful, and most abiding love, the love of a forgiven sinner. The greatest scenes of the Bible, what are they? They are the scenes of repentance and forgiveness: Joseph in the Court of Pharaoh forgiving and weeping over those cruel brothers who had sold him for a slave and broken his father's heart; David repenting of his sin and hearing the prophet Nathan say, "The Lord also hath put away thy sin"; the prodigal son coming back, gaunt and ragged and diseased from the far country, and being greeted with his father's kiss; Peter, who had cursed his Lord, now standing there by the glowing embers of the fire on the Sea of Galilee and hearing Jesus ask him, "Lovest thou me?" Paul, bloody fanatic and persecutor, repenting of his sins and saying to Jesus, "Lord, what wilt thou have me to do?" And that poor thief on the cross, his naked body covered with blood, the darkness of death coming down over him, turning to Jesus and praying, "Lord, remember me when thou comest into thy kingdom," and hearing that last great answer of Jesus, "Today shalt thou be with me in paradise!" Side by side with those great scenes, and as wonderful and as moving as any, stands this one, where Christ forgave the woman who was a sinner and who had washed His feet with her tears and dried them with the hairs of her head.

It would be a mistake to think that this was the first meeting between Jesus and the woman. If that had been so, then there would have been no meaning in what Jesus said to Simon about her, "To whom little is forgiven, the same loveth little." No; you can count on that; there had been another meeting between them. Standing perhaps on the fringe of the crowd one day as He was preaching, she had heard Him say, "Blessed are they which do hunger and thirst after righteousness," or, "Blessed are the pure in heart: for they shall see God," or had heard Him tell one of those parables about a lost sheep or a lost son. In some way, in some place, she had found her way to

Christ; He had spoken to her the words of life, and to Him she had made her confession of faith.

There has been a vast amount of talking and writing and debating about Jesus Christ, about the application of His principles to human society, about His place in history, about His influence upon human lives—a vast amount of that—and yet the single tear of a penitent, a forgiven sinner like this woman will tell you more about Christ and His person and His kingdom and His power and His redeeming love than all those others put together. She loved much, for she had been forgiven much.

As this wonderful interview came to an end, Jesus said to the woman, "Go in peace." The woman must now go back from the light of that banqueting hall, from the close presence of the Savior, from the touch of her hand upon His feet, from His kind and generous words of appreciation and of commendation and of forgiveness; back now to the old, hard world, her beauty still her danger and temptation, for all about her were those who would still try to keep her a sinner. But Jesus said to her, and there is the ring of authority and assurance in His voice, "Go in peace. You have My peace in your heart. That will protect you from the temptations of wicked men. That peace will be your companion in lonely hours. That peace will be a lamp to your feet and a light to your path. In the dark places of your life it will be a light which will shine more and more and burn brighter and brighter unto the perfect day when I shall speak with you again in My kingdom. Your faith has saved you. Go in peace."

# 11

## WITH A JUDGE

Before Pontius Pilate (1 Tim. 6:13).

Before the judgment seat of Christ (Rom. 14:10).

He is guilty of death!" That was the verdict brought in by the council that had tried Jesus before Caiaphas, the high priest.

The priests and the scribes and Pharisees, exulting that the end of their enemy was at hand, led Jesus bound through the streets of Jerusalem to the Praetorium, the palace of the governor. This palace, built by Herod the Great, had a splendor and magnificence that was in keeping with all the buildings erected by Herod, famous as a builder as he was infamous in iniquity. As they passed through the streets of the city in the early hours of the morning, the word spread that Jesus had been sentenced to death by the Sanhedrin. People came out of their homes and joined the procession. Many pilgrims who had come to Jerusalem for the feast of the Passover swelled the ranks of the crowd, until when they arrived at the gates of the palace, there was no small multitude.

In his splendid chamber Pilate was asleep on his couch. Before his door lay a Roman soldier. None could pass into the chamber of Pilate without disturbing him. In the hallway outside sentinels marched up and down, and other soldiers kept their stations at the head and the foot of the grand stairway. Pilate was taking no chances with assassination, for he well knew the enmity that the

101

Jews bore to him for his scornful and ruthless administration. The officer on watch at the palace, seeing the crowd gather outside and learning what they wanted, went to the chamber of Pilate and, awakening him, told him that the Jews had brought a prisoner and that they were clamoring for immediate trial. Pilate raised himself on his pillow and with a look of irritation and contempt on his face cried out, "These execrable Jews! Would that I could shed the blood of all of them, as when I mingled the blood of the Galileans with the blood of their sacrifices in the temple! Were it not for the restraint of the Emperor, I would drive them all out of the land. Let the Jews be accursed! Tell them to come with their prisoner at eleven o'clock in the morning. Never again disturb me at this untimely hour."

"But, your lordship," said the centurion, "this seems to be no ordinary accusation or prisoner. A great crowd has assembled. Many of the pilgrims here for the Passover have joined them. The prisoner has been brought from the Sanhedrin; Caiaphas and the high priests and all the notable Jews are here. Lest it causes your lordship trouble, I humbly advise that you hear the case at once."

"Tell them to wait then," said Pilate, "and soon I shall be down on the judgment seat." With that he threw the rich coverings aside and, calling his slave, was washed, shaved, anointed, and clad in his white and purple robes of office. With his governor's baton in his hand he descended the stairway and entered the judgment hall, a noble room at one end of which was the high judgment seat. Pilate ascended the marble steps and seated himself on the lofty sedile. Then he turned to the centurion and said, "Bring in those Jews and their prisoner." The centurion saluted and went to the crowd standing outside the palace gates. In a few minutes he returned to the empty judgment hall and, going up to Pilate, said, "Your lordship, they refuse to come in." "Why?" said Pilate. "Because this is their feast, and they claim that they defile themselves if they enter a house or building of the Gentiles."

"A plague upon them and their foolish superstitions!" exclaimed Pilate. "The bloodthirsty knaves would not hesitate to cut a man's throat, and yet they have scruples about coming into a building! Well, then, I must go out to them."

In front of the palace was the outdoor judgment seat which was not infrequently used. It had two names: one was the Gabatha, for it stood on an elevation, the Roman law requiring that in every trial the accused must be in a place where he could be seen and where others could see him; the other name was the Pavement, for the ground on which the judgment throne was erected was paved with a mosaic of richly colored stones. Leading up to the judgment seat were white marble steps. On the platform stood the procurator's chair, in this case perhaps the golden chair of Archelaeus, the high priest who had been murdered by his brother-in-law, Herod the Great. Everything was in keeping with the dignity and the splendor of the Roman Empire. On either side of the governor's chair were the familiar insignia of Roman power and the four letters, S.P.Q.R., "The Roman Senate and People."

Presently the great doors into the palace swung open, and Pilate, flanked by two guards, came out, a scowl on his countenance as he viewed the excited multitude and, mounting the stairway at the back, seated himself on the golden chair. Then he turned to the officer at his side and said, "Call the prisoner!" At that Jesus was led halfway up the marble stairs, where He stood with His hands bound behind His back. His face showed the anguish through which He had passed in Gethsemane and in the judgment hall of Caiaphas. Plainly discernible, too, were the marks of the blows of those who had struck Him with their fists at His last trial, when they had blindfolded Him and then in cruel mockery had asked Him to prophesy and tell which of them had smitten Him.

Pilate looked now for the first time on the face of Jesus, with whom his name henceforth will be associated to the end of time. "He suffered under Pontius Pilate." In that moment Pilate knew that Jesus was an innocent man, and not an ordinary man. Pilate himself was bad and vicious, a "javelin" man, worthy of his name. Yet as Pilate faced the new prisoner, Jesus spoke to the better man in Pilate and called to him to come forth. There is a godlike man even in the lowest of human beings, for the simple and profound reason that that soul was created in the image of God.

> Down in the human heart,
> Crushed by the tempter,
> Feelings he buried that grace can restore.

That first look of Pilate upon the face of Jesus not only awakened whatever of good there was in him, but it also marked the beginning of a battle between good and evil for the mastery of the soul; a battle such as seldom has been waged. I like to visit old battlefields: Philippi, where Octavius and Mark Antony conquered Brutus and Cassius; Marathon, where the Greeks defeated the Persians; Waterloo, where Napoleon's empire crumbled; Bannockburn, where Bruce defeated the English. But here is a greater battlefield and a greater battle, the battlefield of a man's soul.

Little could Pilate have foreseen that such a day would ever come for him. Little could he have known, when the centurion aroused him out of his slumber that gray Friday morning, that this was to be the day of destiny for him. If I could tell you that at ten o'clock tomorrow you would be confronted with a certain temptation, you would have time to prepare yourself against it. But that is not the way temptation comes. It comes suddenly, unexpectedly, like a thief in the night. "Therefore be ye also ready," Christ says, "for in such an hour as ye think not the Son of man cometh." So it is with the great temptations of life. We never know when they are coming. Therefore watch and pray, that you may be ready in the day of battle.

THE QUESTIONING

After gazing in silence for a little at Jesus, as He stood there before him, Pilate called out in a ringing, commanding, Roman voice, "What accusation bring ye against this man?" The answer came, spoken, no doubt, by Caiaphas, the high priest, with a half-disguised tone of insolence, "If he were not a malefactor, we would not have delivered him up unto thee." Then at once those who stood around in the crowd took up the cry and flung their accusations against Jesus, "He perverts the people! He forbids them to give tribute to Caesar! He says that He Himself is a king! He says He can tear down the temple and build it again in three days!" And others cried, "He breaks the law of Moses and dishonors the traditions of our people!"

In answer to this chorus of accusation Pilate said haughtily and scornfully, "Take him yourselves and judge him according to your law. You have a law. Why do you come here to bother me?" The high priest answered, "It is not lawful for us to put any man to death." That gave Pilate a start. It let him know for the first time that this was a capital case and that the council had already found Jesus guilty, worthy of death. In ordinary circumstances Pilate might have given a quick and formal ratification to their verdict. But when he looked upon Jesus, he hesitated.

Speaking to the officers at his side again, Pilate said, "Bring the prisoner inside to my judgment chambers." Then he descended from the judgment throne and once more entered the palace. When Jesus stood before him Pilate said, "Art thou the King of the Jews? Is this true what they say, that you claim to be a king?" To this Jesus answered, "Sayest thou this thing of thyself, or did others tell it thee of me?" Pilate answered with a touch of scorn, "Am I a Jew? Do you suppose that I know or care anything about these Jewish squabbles over their religion or over their puppet king? Your own people have delivered you to me. Now tell me, what have you done?"

Jesus answered, "My kingdom is not of this world: if my kingdom were of this world, then would my servants fight, that I should not be delivered to the Jews: but now is my kingdom not from hence." Impressed with the fact that Jesus again used the word "kingdom" and therefore must claim to be a king, Pilate, half in doubt and half perhaps in irony, said, "Art thou a king then?" Jesus replied, "To this end was I born, and for this cause came I into the world, that I should bear witness unto the truth." It was as if He had said, "Yes; I am a king. But my kingdom, unlike that of Rome, is a kingdom of God, a kingdom of truth."

"Truth!" said Pilate, as he arose from his ivory chair and strode up and down. "'What is truth?' said jesting Pilate, and would not stay for the answer," wrote Francis Bacon in his famous essay. I wonder if Pilate was only jesting. Perhaps there was a tone of bitterness in his words, as if to say, "In this world of sham and cruelty and greed and lust and appetite, where and what is truth?" And there, unknown to Pilate, standing bound before him, stood Truth Himself!

## The Subterfuge

Pilate did not stay long to hear what Jesus might have said as to the nature of truth, but striking on the marble pavement with his procurator's rod, he summoned the centurion again and said, "Take the prisoner out." This time, instead of going out himself, Pilate went up to a balcony between the pillars of the palace and, pointing down to Jesus who stood before the judgment seat, called out to the crowd, "I find no fault—" But before he could finish the sentence angry shouts went up: "He is a blasphemer!" "He perverts the people!" "He would destroy the temple!" "Let Him be crucified." "He stirreth up the people, throughout all Jewry, beginning from Galilee to this place!" Pilate caught at that. There perhaps was a way of escape for him. If Jesus was a Galilean, He ought to be judged by the ruler of that country, Herod Antipas, and off to Herod he sent Him.

Herod had long wanted to see Jesus. Once his guilty conscience had made him fear that Jesus was John the Baptist risen from the dead. But whatever questions Herod asked when Jesus came before him, Jesus answered not a word. Unwilling to load his troubled conscious with the guilt of another murder, Herod mocked Him and sent Him back to Pilate. Pilate was not able to turn his responsibility over to another. Your wife, your husband, your friend, your associate, your minister—none of them can take your place. You are the one who must decide.

Pilate, congratulating himself now that he was rid of this troublesome case, had hardly finished his breakfast when an officer came in to report to him, saying that the prisoner Jesus was again outside the palace gates; that Herod refused to try Him and had only mocked Him and robed Him in a gorgeous garment and sent Him back. Once more Pilate went out and ascended his judgment seat. As he did so the soldiers who stood in a circle about the pavement, seeing that the crowd was getting somewhat out of hand, took their long spears and, holding them horizontally in front of them, roughly pushed the mob back, clearing the space about the judgment seat.

As he looked again upon Jesus, Pilate suddenly remembered that one of his privileges as governor was to show good will to the people by releasing to them at the time of the Passover any prisoner for whom they should ask. There happened to be in the jail at that time a notorious criminal, Barabbas, guilty of insurrection and murder. In some uprising against the Roman authorities Barabbas had gained a little popularity with the people. When Pilate said to the crowd, "Will ye therefore that I release unto you the King of the Jews?" they answered with a great roar, "No! Not this man, but Barabbas!" The fact that Pilate asked this question and imagined, even for a moment, that the bloodthirsty crowd before him would rather see Jesus released than Barabbas, shows how distraught he was. He had asked the people for their will and they had expressed it. Pilate gave a curt order to one of the officers, and presently Barabbas was led out of his prison. When the mob saw him a great shout of jubilation went up. Barabbas took his stand with the others and joined with them in taunting the prisoner whose condemnation meant his own freedom.

### THE WARNING

Pilate was still troubled and perplexed. Every move that he had made to set Jesus free had been blocked. But just at that moment there was granted to him another chance, that truce of God so often granted to tempted and troubled souls. In her luxurious bedroom Pilate's wife, Claudia Procula, awakened out of a troubled sleep. She called her maid and said to her, "Julia, I have had a terrible dream. In my dream I saw an innocent man, and a noble spirit he seemed to be. He was on trial before my lord Pilate and was sentenced to death. Immediately there were signs and omens of evil in the heaven and the earth. A weight, intolerable and indescribable, rested upon my soul. And in my dream I saw my lord Pilate with a look of anguish and remorse upon his countenance, wandering to and fro and up and down in the earth, and whenever he came to a river or a fountain where there was water he put his hands into the water and began to wash them, and then he would hold them up and look hopelessly upon them as if he still saw there the stain which he had vainly sought to wash out. What think you, Julia, what could such a dream be?"

"I do not know, mistress," answered Julia; "but what you have told me frightens me, too."

"Hark! What is that?" exclaimed Claudia. The roar of the mob came through the open casement, "Crucify him! Crucify him!" Julia ran to the window and called back to her mistress, "The Procurator is on the judgment seat, and before him stands a prisoner bound. Perhaps that may be the prisoner of whom my mistress dreamed?"

"Yes, it may be," said Claudia. Calling for a stylus and a parchment, she hastily wrote a message to Pilate. Another slave carried it out and gave it to the centurion, who put it into the hand of Pilate as he sat there, troubled and vexed and perplexed, on the judgment seat. Pilate unrolled the parchment and read the message from his wife, "Have thou nothing to do with that just man: for I have suffered many things this day in a dream because of him."

"Yes," Pilate said to himself; "He is indeed a just man. What I felt when first my eye fell upon Him, what I felt when I examined Him in private, and what I felt when I heard the angry shouts of His bloodthirsty accusers is now confirmed by the gods themselves. This dream of Claudia tells me that He is an innocent man and warns me not to give Him over to His enemies." So saying, he crumpled the parchment in his hand and threw it behind him.

But how to get Him free? How to deliver Him out of the hands of this mob and yet not have an insurrection on his own hands, that was the problem. Then he bethought himself of one more possibility. "Perhaps if I order him to be scourged," said Pilate, "that will satisfy them, and I can let Him go. . . . Take the prisoner and scourge Him," he said to the centurion. At a word from the centurion two soldiers took Jesus between them into the prison room of the palace. We shall not linger long in that terrible room. Had it been Barabbas himself who had been scourged, we could hardly endure the sight of it; this was Jesus, who had taken little children up in His arms and blessed them. The soldiers stripped Him of His garments, and then, wielding their whips of leather thongs, the ends of which were loaded with iron, they began to strike Him. The cruel blows quickly brought blood as the iron-loaded thongs bit into His flesh. Then they took a bough of thorns, twisted it into a circle, and pressed it down upon His head. After that they took the crimson robe that Pilate had mockingly given Him and placed it over His shoulders, first applying some rude remedy to staunch a little the flow of blood, lest the beaten man die on their hands and they have to answer to Pilate for it.

## THE VERDICT

So Jesus was led out once more, and again He took His stand before the judgment seat, the blood from His wounds staining red the white marble steps. Pointing to Jesus, and still hoping that this would satisfy them, Pilate cried out, "Behold the man! I find no fault in him!" But the mob flung back their wild answer, "Crucify him! Crucify him!"

But still Pilate hesitated. He could not bring himself to say the dreadful word, "Guilty," and order the soldiers to crucify Jesus. As he hesitated, he heard someone in the crowd cry out in a strident tone, "If thou let this man go, thou art not Caesar's friend: whosoever maketh himself a king speaketh against Caesar." When Pilate heard that, he received his mortal wound. Caesar's friend! He had not thought of that. If he let Jesus go, the Jews threatened to tell Caesar that he had set free a man who was conspiring and plotting to be Caesar himself. To incur the wrath of any Caesar, particularly that of the gloomy Tiberius, would be a fearful thing. It would mean the loss of his governorship, the loss of his palaces and villas, his princely income, his stables and yachts, his friends and mistresses, and probably life itself. "Thou art not Caesar's friend!" That settled it. The battle was over. "Their voices prevailed." Pilate gave the order, "Take ye him, and crucify him." He made one more feeble effort, however, for before he gave the final word he said, "Shall I crucify your King?" Immediately the shout went up, "We have no king but Caesar!" Again rose that terrible specter, Tiberius Caesar. When Pilate thought of him he surrendered. "Then he delivered him therefore unto them to be crucified."

The battle was over, and Pilate had lost. Satan had won. There was another act, however, an unforgettable one in this great drama of Pilate and Jesus. Pilate called for a basin of water and, washing his hands in it before the multitude, said, "I am innocent of the blood of this just person: see ye to it." The people shouted that they would see to it, and that they gladly would let the blood of this Man be on them and on their children. But as Pilate left them, I imagine he looked at his hands and saw that they were red with blood which no water could ever wash away.

What a drama that was—Pilate struggling for his soul; his reason, his judgment, his fears, his superstition all urging him to do the right; yet over all these obstacles and warnings he marched on to his great crime and henceforth will be known forever as that "Pontius Pilate under whom Jesus suffered."

We have been looking at Jesus standing before the judgment seat of Pilate; but as we have been describing that scene, I have felt, and I am sure you have felt, that the real scene, the real trial is different. It is not Jesus before Pilate, but Pilate standing where we must all stand, before the judgment seat of Christ.

It took Pilate a long time to reach his decision about Jesus. But when he had once made it, it was final. There was no recalling of it. He had ordered written over the cross, "Jesus of Nazareth, the King of the Jews." The Jews asked him to alter that inscription and make it read, "He said, I am King of the Jews." But Pilate, altogether unhappy now, answered in anger, "What I have written, I have written."

That was true concerning the inscription which the Jews wanted altered. It was a half confession, too, that he believed that Jesus was the King of the Jews. But it was true also in another sense. The verdict which Pilate had written about Jesus, the verdict of condemnation and of rejection was now final. What he had written he had written.

Everyone of us writes the final verdict of his own soul

concerning Jesus. However we may debate and discuss, evade or postpone, at length comes the verdict which must stand forever and which we must face when we stand before the judgment seat of Christ. Is your verdict about Christ the one that you really desire to be the final one, the one that cannot be reversed, the one that will confront you as your final, irrevocable decision about Christ, when, instead of Christ standing before you and awaiting your verdict, you stand before Christ to await His verdict?

# 12

## WITH A MAN WHO KNEW WHAT HE WANTED

What wilt thou that I should do unto thee? (Mark 10:51).

Would you rather be blind or deaf? One might say, "I would rather be deaf than blind, for then I could still see." But if you were deaf you would never hear the sigh of the wind in the tops of the trees on a summer evening, like the sigh of infinite pity and sadness. You would never hear the breaking of the waves on the seashore, like the voice of eternity. You would never hear the matins of the birds or the voice of the orator or the voices of the mother and her little child or the whisper of a lover or the voice of the great congregation uplifted in praise of the triune God.

Another might say, "I would rather be blind than deaf for then I could still hear the human voice and communicate with my fellow man." But if you were blind, think of what you would never see: the waving blossoms on the trees in the springtime, the blue sky and the sun rejoicing as a strong man to run a race, or the stars and the moon at night. You would never see the light in a lover's eyes; you would never look on the ocean rolling as it has rolled in splendor since Creation's dawn.

We are concerned with a man who was blind, and not only blind but poor, a dark spot in the sunlight of life, a sort of question mark on the wisdom and goodness of God. From the darkness of his mother's womb he passed into the darkness of this world. Blindness has always evoked a degree of pity. Blind men as they appear in literature are either very bad or very good—bad like Pew, the blind seaman of *Treasure Island*, or good like Nydia, Bulwer-Lytton's lovely character in *The Last Days of Pompeii*. Blind men evoked the pity of Jesus, for we know that He opened the eyes of at least five of them: two others here at Jericho, one at Bethsaida, and the man who washed in the pool of Siloam.

It was springtime in Palestine, but there was no springtime for this blind man, Bartimaeus. For him winter and summer, spring and autumn were all the same. He did not even have a name. Mark calls him Bartimaeus, but all that means is that he was the son of a man named Timaeus. What his own name was, if he had one, no one knew or cared.

Morning dawned over the tawny houses and walls of Jericho. The blind man emerged from the stable where he had slept, shook the straw from his shabby garments, and tapping his way with his cane, moved on by his familiar beat toward the gate of Jericho. Perhaps he was able to beg a drink of milk from a woman who was milking her goat, and then a crust of bread to go with it. Slowly he moved, going down that alley and up this street until he had made his way out through the main gate of Jericho and sat down in his familiar place against the wall, drawing his shabby robe close about him, for although it was springtime, the morning air was sharp and piercing.

There he sat, wondering what good or bad luck the day would bring him. He heard the prelude to the chorus of the day's traffic. Here came a donkey loaded with melons for the market; after the donkey a woman, several women, with pitchers on their heads, coming from the fountain back to the toil of their houses; then a woman with an enormous heap of sticks on her head; then several soft-footed camels, swaying under their load of Araby's spices; then a donkey laden with fish for the market in Jerusalem. So they passed, and Bartimaeus put up his plaintive but unheeded cry for alms.

Suddenly the beggar lifted up his head in an alert posture, for with his practiced ear he had heard the approach of an unusual procession, the hum of a great crowd, the shuffling of many feet. First of all came the boys, running before the crowd with their shrill cries; then the people hurried past him as they came out of the gate of Jericho to see what was going on. Bartimaeus listened intently for a little and then, reaching out his hand, seized the skirt of a passerby, detained him for a moment and called out, "What is the excitement? Where are all the people going? Who are they running to see?" Snatching the skirt out of his grasp, the passerby hurried on, but as he went he called over his shoulder to Bartimaeus, "Jesus of Nazareth is passing by!" Do not forget that man who told Bartimaeus the news. If he had not told him, Bartimaeus might never have known that day that Jesus was near.

"Jesus of Nazareth!" Bartimaeus said to himself. "Where have I heard that name before? Ah, yes. Isn't He the prophet that a kind man who once stopped here at the gate spoke of, telling me that this Jesus had healed the sick and cleansed the leper and had even opened the eyes of a blind man? Yes; I am sure that is the name, Jesus of Nazareth! I understand that none of our rulers or the scribes or Pharisees like Him. They call Him an evildoer, an impostor. And yet if He takes pity on the poor and the sick, as I have heard He does, He can't be such a bad man. Some say He is the Messiah. Once in the synagogue, too, I remember a scribe reading from the scroll of Isaiah how the Messiah when He came would open the eyes of the blind. What if He could open my eyes! How wonderful it would be to be able to see, to walk in any direction I wanted to instead of just this same monotonous beat every day—out of the barn, down the alley, up the street, and out of the gate! How wonderful it would be to see the faces of other people and see the sky that I have heard men talk of! Perhaps He can open my eyes too!"

## THE CRY FOR MERCY

Then he thought to himself, "But I am only a beggar. I would have nothing to pay Him, even if He did heal me. They say, too, that He is passing by, that He is leaving the city; He probably wouldn't have time for me. Anyway the rulers and important people around Him would never let me come near

Him. There is none to guide me to Him. How could I ever get through the crowd? And yet, what if He could open my eyes! At least I will ask Him!" With that he lifted up his voice, "Jesus, thou son of David, have mercy on me!" The man whose skirt he had seized a moment before had said only, "Jesus of Nazareth," but Bartimaeus added to that. He had heard that this man claimed to be the Messiah, and so when he cried out he gave Him a title: "Jesus, thou son of David, have mercy on me." He did not expect that Jesus would heal him and open his eyes simply because He had the power or simply because He was asked to do it, but Bartimaeus had faith that in His great goodness Jesus would have mercy upon him.

As soon as Bartimaeus began to cry out, the other beggars ordered him to be silent. "Close your mouth, Bartimaeus! Don't be a fool! If you make a noise like that, the magistrates will order us to be beaten and cast us into the prison." Some of the citizens, too, who stood around told him to be silent. "Keep still, Bartimaeus! Who wants to hear anything from a beggar like you when the great prophet is going by?"

None ever came to Christ without someone trying to stop him. It is bad enough not to come ourselves but still worse to hinder others. Ask yourself, "Have I ever helped anyone to Christ? If I have not done that, then have I ever hindered one from coming?" Are there any words, any deeds, any disposition in you which have hindered or are now hindering another from coming to Christ? Will that be held against you in the Day of Judgment?

But the more they rebuked Bartimaeus, the more he cried out. "Many charged him that he should hold his peace." But he cared nothing for that. If a man is going to come to Christ, he must overcome his own obstacles and doubts and fears and also the obstacles that others place in his path. Christ had awakened the great hope and yearning in the beggar's breast. "Jesus, thou son of David, have mercy on me."

## THE KINDNESS OF CHRIST

"And Jesus stood still." People wonder about the sun standing still in Joshua's great battle. But here is something more wonderful: the Son of God Himself stood still. He stopped on His way to Calvary to heed a beggar's cry. Christ heard; He always hears. And when He hears, He always stops. One morning in Capernaum's street the people pressed upon Him, hundreds of them, touching Him, but when He felt the touch on the hem of His garment by that woman who was sick, immediately He stopped. "Jesus stood still." When Jesus stops, something is sure to happen.

As soon as He stopped, the important people about Him began to make apologies for the beggar's loud interruption. They had given strict orders that all beggars should be kept off the line of march. "We are sorry, indeed, that our orders have not been—" But Jesus interrupted them, "Call him! Call him!" You can see the look of surprise in their faces. He had stopped to call a beggar, that miserable, blind beggar, blind Bartimaeus! But there was no doubt about it. Jesus said, "Call him." So they ran to where Bartimaeus was sitting there against the wall and said, "Be of good comfort, rise; he calleth thee."

You can imagine the thrill of Bartimaeus when he heard that. It was the first time in his life that anyone had wanted him or had called to him. He was always wanting something, calling to someone to do something for him. All that he had heard hitherto was, "Be gone! Get out of my way! Take yourself off, you noisy beggar!" But now it was different, "Rise; he calleth thee!" The very people who a moment before had been telling Bartimaeus to close his mouth and suppress his loud cries went out of their way to show him attention. One stretched out his hand to him. Another said, "Here is your staff," and another, "Here is your robe." But before they could help him, Bartimaeus sprang up himself, threw his staff in one direction and his old worm-eaten robe in the other, and as all opened up a way for him, ran to Jesus.

There they stood now, face-to-face, Bartimaeus all atremble, all athrill. What a picture to paint! Angels, come down and paint it for me if you will! Let me see the look on the face of Jesus! Let me see the look on the face of Bartimaeus! Let me see the look on the face of Peter and Thomas and John and the rulers and the crowd as they stand about, expecting to see a great miracle. And they are not going to be disappointed.

Divine power and compassion are now face-to-face with human need.

What did Jesus do? What did He say? He said to the blind man, "What wilt thou that I should do unto thee?" Why did Jesus ask that? He must have known that the man was blind. Did He do it to calm Bartimaeus? Did He do it to let all who stood about and perhaps could not see what was going on know that He was going to work a miracle and open the blind man's eyes? Whatever the reason was, He said, "Bartimaeus, what wilt thou that I should do unto thee?"

Here was a beggar who knew. What did he ask for? What did he say? Here was One who could do anything for him. Did he say, "Lord, give me a warm robe for these rags"? Did he say, "Give me a house instead of a barn to sleep in"? Did he say, "Make me a ruler of the people"? Did he say, "Give me a good-paying job like that of Zacchaeus"? Did he say, "Give me plenty of money and plenty of food"? No; he asked for none of these things. He asked for the greatest thing of all: "Lord, that I might receive my sight." And Jesus said, "Go thy way; thy faith hath made thee whole." And immediately he received his sight.

## THE GREATEST OF ALL SIGHTS

Think of what Bartimaeus saw. Think of the wonders of seeing for the first time a crowd of human beings just like himself, the walls and palm tree groves of Jericho, the sky so blue above him, and the hills of Moab in the distance. But that was not the first thing that he saw. The first thing was the face of Jesus, the face of the One who had healed him. And for you and me, too, that will be the greatest of all sights. When we awake from the dream men call life, when we put off the image of the earth and break the bonds of time and mortality, when the scales of time and sense have fallen from our eyes and the garment of corruption has been put off, when this mortality has put on immortality and this corruption has put on incorruption and we awaken in the everlasting morning, that will be the sight that will stir us and hold us. Oh, I am sure there will be many wonderful sights there—the sea of glass mingled with fire, the great white throne, the river of water of life, and the tree of life that yielded her fruit every season; those marvelous twelve gates, every gate a pearl; those marvelous foundations of the walls, garnished with all manner of precious stones; the faces of the patriarchs and the prophets and the apostles and the martyrs; the faces of those we have loved long since and lost awhile. But most wonderful of all will be the face into which Bartimaeus looked that morning outside the gate of Jericho after his eyes had been opened, the face of Him who loved us and redeemed us and washed us from our sins in His own precious blood.

## THE POWER OF THE WILL

Here was a man who knew what he wanted and got what he asked for. He knew that he was blind, and he asked to see. God gave him the "seeing eye." If Christ were present now as He was in Jericho of old—No; I will not put it that way, for Christ is always here, as truly as He was that morning at Jericho. I will put it this way: If your eyes were opened to see that He is really here, and if He gave you the hearing ear so that you could hear Him say, "What wilt thou that I should do unto thee," what would you will? It is the power of will that wins the prizes of this life and also of eternal life. What will you then that Christ should do for you? Do not be general and vague, but make it specific. If the truth were told, would many not need to ask something like this: "Lord, that I might have a kind and Christian tongue." "Lord, that I might be able to keep my temper." "Lord, that I might be delivered from rash judgment and criticism of others." "Lord, that the poison of hate and jealousy might be drawn from my heart." "Lord, that the pool of my imagination might be cleansed." "Lord, that the chain of this evil habit might be broken." "Lord, that the fear of tomorrow or the memory of yesterday might be lifted from me." "Lord, that I might get the victory over this besetting sin or this dangerous temptation." "Lord, that I might have strength to bear this sore trial and carry this heavy burden."

Jesus of Nazareth is passing by, but He will stop for you if you ask Him. He says to you now, "What wilt thou that I should do unto thee?" All our needs are summed up in that one great need of eternal life which we have in Christ. He who stopped in Jericho streets can still bestow His power and His healing upon the man who has faith, for He said to that beggar, "Thy faith hath made thee whole."

Jesus of Nazareth is passing by. Suppose that when Bartimaeus heard these words he had said to himself, "I will not call on Him today. I will wait until the crowd is gone and there will be no one to rebuke me or hold me back." Or, "I will wait until I hear more of what the scribes and Pharisees and rabbis have to say about His claims." Or, "I will wait until He comes to Jericho again." If he had done that, Bartimaeus would never have had his eyes opened, for Jesus was going out of Jericho for the last time on His way to Jerusalem, on His way to die on Calvary. That first chance of Bartimaeus was also his last, and when he heard that Jesus was passing, he called on Him.

Again Jesus of Nazareth is passing by! "He calleth for you." Only once He called for Bartimaeus, and immediately Bartimaeus ran to Him. Many times He has called for you, but you have not yet come to Him. Be of good courage. Rise up, He calls for you—you with your burden of care, you on your sick bed, you with your crushed hope, you with your disappointment, you with your loneliness, you with your temptation, you with your burden of sin. He calls for you! He stopped once and stood still for Bartimaeus. He will stop for you. Jesus of Nazareth is passing by.

# 13

## WITH A MAN WHO CURSED HIM

Thou knowest that I love thee (John 21:17).

Seven men in a ship. The ship at anchor with a little boat fastened to the stern. Both ship and boat are rising and falling with the gentle pulsation of the sea. The darkness is fading away before the dawn as it has done ever since the first night and the first morning. The mists that have covered the sea are beginning to lift. Far to the east the gray mountains of Gadara begin to show themselves. To the west are the red roofs of the houses of Tiberias. The sea is heaving gently like the breast of a sleeping woman. The little waves are washing softly on the stones and pebbles of the beach. In the distance other boats appear in the gray light of the morning with other fishermen plying their trade.

Seven men in a ship. The names of five of them are Peter, Thomas, Nathanael, and the two brothers, James and John. There are two others there whose names we do not know. One of them, I feel sure, must be Andrew and the other perhaps Philip. All of them are naked save for a loincloth, for they have been doing the rough and dirty work of the sea. They look weary and a little discouraged, too, for they have been fishing all night and have caught nothing. Now the brown nets hang awash over the gunwale. In the waist of the ship, gasping and floundering about, are two or three small fish, the fruit of their long toil. Thomas says, "All night we've been at it with the sail and the

120

oars and the net, lowering and dragging and then pulling in again, and this is all we have to show for it, these two or three flounders!" With a gesture of contempt he reaches down, takes them by the tail, and flings them back into the sea.

But Andrew says, "Let us give it another trial. Let us put down the net once more. Perhaps we shall have better luck this time." James has thrown out a line with a hook on it, thinking he may make a catch that way. The leader of them, Peter, the one who suggested this fishing expedition when the disciples came back to Galilee from Jerusalem after the resurrection of Jesus, stands irresolute in the middle of the ship, his hand grasping the mast. The others wonder what Peter will say.

As they are waiting a voice hails them from the distance, "Children, have you caught any fish?" Turning, they see standing on the distant shore, still half-enveloped in the morning mists, someone who they suppose is just another fisherman. Peter puts his hand to his mouth and shouts over the sea an emphatic and loud-sounding No! Then the Stranger on the shore calls back to them, "Try it on the other side of the ship, and you will have better luck." Peter and the rest of them think that this Stranger has discerned a shadow which tells of an approaching shoal of fish. At any rate it will do no harm to try once more. "Overboard, boys, with the net!" Peter calls James and John and Thomas and all the rest of them to lend a hand, and over the net goes.

Meanwhile, John has been looking intently toward the shore where the Stranger is standing with the glow of a kindled fire beside Him, the spiral of smoke going up toward the sky. As the rest of the fishermen are pulling in the net, now filled with a big catch, John says, "Peter, it is the Lord!" At that Peter straightens himself up and says, "Are you sure?" at the same time putting his hand to his eyes and looking intently toward the shore. "Yes," answers John, "it is He!" With that Peter turns and cries, "Thomas, hand me that cloak!" Thomas reaches him his cloak and, fastening it about his naked body, Peter leaps overboard with a splash; as he strikes out for shore with powerful strokes, he turns his head for a moment toward the boat and calls out, "John, you beat me that morning of the Resurrection when we ran together to the sepulcher, but this is the time I will beat you!" He is thinking, too, of another time when he knew that the Lord was near, jumped overboard, and tried to get to Jesus in a hurry. This time he is more successful. Soon he has come in far enough to touch bottom, and now, eagerly and rapidly, he is walking up the shore toward the place where Jesus is standing. The others in the ship have pulled up the anchor, fastened the net astern, and with their oars are bringing the ship in not far behind Peter. Soon they can anchor the ship again and, jumping into the small boat, skull their way to the shore.

Near where Jesus stands, a fire is burning briskly, and on the coals lie several fish. What is more cheerful in the early cool morning, after a night of toil, than a glowing fire? And what is more tasty to hungry men in the early morning than a freshly cooked fish? As they gather around the fire Jesus says, "Bring in the fish which you caught in the net." At that Peter goes down into the sea again, wades out to the anchored ship, looses the fastenings of the net, and with the help of some of the others drags it up on the beach. And there they are! A hundred and fifty-three of them! Big, splendid, silver fish, flashing in the morning sunlight as they leap up and down in the net.

When the fish have been made secure, Jesus says to the disciples, "Come and dine." Accepting His invitation, they all gather about the fire and sit down. Jesus, after He has given thanks, takes the bread and the fish and distributes them among the disciples. Peter must have been thinking of the last time he sat about a fire warming himself when his Lord came near. That was the night he had sworn and cursed and said he had never known Jesus. How different it is now. Save for an occasional remark about the catch of fish or the sea, no one says anything. It is a silent meal. They all know who He is, and yet they hesitate to ask Him for a confirmation of their belief. As John puts it, "None of the disciples durst ask Him, Who art thou? Knowing that it was the Lord."

PETER RESTORED

When the meal was finished, Jesus began to speak to Peter. There was no one of the disciples who talked so often to Jesus and no one of them with whom Jesus talked so often. This was the last of those remarkable interviews which began when his brother Andrew brought Peter to Christ and Jesus said, "Thou art Simon the son of Jona: thou shalt be called Cephas, which is by interpretation, a stone."

There were four steps in the restoration of Peter after his terrible and shameful fall. The first was that marvelous look Jesus gave Peter when He was being led away from the court of Caiaphas and He heard Peter cursing Him. The second was the message which the women who had gone to the tomb early in the morning had brought to him, for the angel had said to them, "Go, tell his disciples and Peter." When Peter heard that, how his heart must have leaped with joy and hope! The next step was that special appearance which Jesus made for Peter. When the two men came back to Jerusalem from Emmaus and told of their wonderful experience with the One who had walked with them on the road, the others answered, "The Lord is risen indeed, and hath appeared to Simon!" Paul, too, mentions that appearance to Peter: "He was seen of Cephas." Of all the resurrection appearances of Jesus, that is the one I would like to know the most about, but it is the very one which we know nothing about. Perhaps the reason is that it was too sacred even for the inspired pens of the evangelists who wrote the Gospels. What a meeting it must have been, that first meeting between Jesus and the disciple who had cursed Him!

Now comes the last step in the restoration of Peter, the interview there by the glowing embers of the fire that morning by the Sea of Galilee. It was indeed an appropriate place for such an interview and restoration. That was the place that Peter knew best; every changing hue of the sky and every mood of the sea, every little bay or indentation, every rock or shoal, every hill and mountain around it was familiar to him. It was there, too, when he was fishing with Andrew and John, that he had first heard Jesus say, "Follow me."

Turning to Peter, Jesus said, using the name by which He had first known him, "Simon, son of Jonas, lovest thou me more than these?" As He spoke He must have motioned with His hand toward the other disciples who sat about the fire listening eagerly to what was being said. "Lovest thou me more than these?" And what did that remind Peter of? He must have thought about that night at the Last Supper when Jesus had said that all the disciples were going to forsake Him, and Peter had said, "Though all men shall be offended because of thee, yet will I never be offended. Though I should die with thee, yet will I not deny thee." That proud saying came back to Peter now as Jesus said to him, pointing to John and James and Thomas and Nathanael and the others, "Lovest thou me more than these?" This time there was no boasting, no quick and easy assurance in Peter's voice. All that he said was in deep humility, "Yea, Lord; thou knowest that I love thee." Jesus said to him, "Feed my lambs." Feed the weak, the ones who are likely to stumble in their discipleship. The weak was to feed the weak! The one who had failed the most dismally was now to keep others from failing!

A second time Jesus said to Peter, "Lovest thou me?" this time making no allusion to the other disciples or to Peter's love as compared with theirs. It was simply, "Lovest thou me?" Again Peter answered, "Yea, Lord; thou knowest that I love thee." Jesus said to him, "Feed my sheep." Then the third time Jesus asked Peter, "Lovest thou me?" This time Peter showed by the look on his face and by the tone of his voice that the third question of Jesus had grieved him. It is the only time we read of Jesus grieving a human soul, for He came not to grieve people but to heal and comfort them. But He was speaking now with a purpose, for Peter's good. Peter answered in his sorrow, "Lord, thou knowest all things; thou knowest that I love thee." It was as if he had said, "Why do you ask me again, Lord, if I love thee? You know my heart, and You know that I love You." And that was true. Jesus did not need to ask Peter to find out whether or not Peter loved Him. He knew what was in Peter's heart, just as He knows what is in your heart.

But for Peter's good and for the good of those other six disciples gathered about the fire, and for our good too, Jesus asked Peter three times to confess his love for Him, just as once before, seated beside another fire, Peter had three times denied that he knew Him or loved Him.

For the third and last time Jesus said to Peter, "Feed my

sheep." Think of that! If He had said it to John or to James or Thomas or Nathanael, there would have been nothing strange about it. But He said it to Peter; Peter who had cursed Him and denied Him; Peter who, when the testing hour came, had shown such cowardice and weakness. Yet it was to that very disciple that Jesus now gave the commission, "Go out and feed my sheep. Bring them back into the fold." That was what He had told Peter once before when He had warned him on the night of his fall and said, "When thou art converted, strengthen thy brethren." Peter was now able to go forth, converted and changed by marvelous love, to feed the sheep of Christ and to strengthen his brethren. In the riches of God's grace, Peter was a greater disciple and a greater preacher because of his fall. That shows the completeness of Christ's forgiveness. If He had said, "Peter, you are forgiven. I will not hold it against you. Your transgression is blotted out. Your iniquity is covered," that would have been one thing. But He said to him, "Feed my sheep." That meant that his forgiveness was complete, that he was not only forgiven but trusted, and that out of his sin and fall and repentance and restoration new power and new grace would come to him.

## PETER AND THE FUTURE

You can imagine the great joy that must have been surging up in Peter's heart when he heard those words, "Feed my sheep." But immediately came a different word, a very sobering one. Jesus said, "Verily, I say unto thee, When thou wast young, thou girdest thyself, and walkedst whither thou wouldest: but when thou shalt be old, thou shalt stretch forth thy hands, and another shall gird thee, and carry thee whither thou wouldest not."

What a change that foretold for Peter! It is almost impossible for us to think of the active, impulsive Peter becoming old. It is almost impossible for us to think of Peter, who had gone his own way whenever he pleased and however he pleased, now girded with ropes and chains and carried where someone else wanted him to go. John tells us that Jesus meant to say that Peter, for the sake of his Master, was going to die a martyr's death. He told Peter, in the very moment He re-stored him and gave him his great commission, that he must follow his Master in the path not only of service and obedience but of trial and suffering and death. He was to say the same thing of Paul at Damascus, "I will show him how great things he must suffer for my name's sake."

When he uttered this prediction, Jesus evidently made a sign to Peter to go apart with Him for a little, for He said, "Follow me." Peter rose up to follow Him, pondering in his mind that word that Jesus had said about his martyrdom and death. Then he heard a step behind him and, looking over his shoulder, saw that John was following him. Peter then said to Jesus, "Lord, and what shall this man do? What about John? What will happen to him? Will he, too, meet the martyr's death?" I do not think that that was a question of idle curios-ity. Peter was deeply attached to John. The relationship be-tween them had been a very close one. They had been together in all the great moments of their Master's ministry. They alone had penetrated the courtyard of Caiaphas when Jesus was on trial there, and after Peter's fall, John had evidently taken him in to his lodgings or his home at Jerusalem, for Peter was with John when the word came that the tomb was empty. No won-der Peter wanted to know what was going to happen to John. "Lord, what shall this man do?"

Jesus answered, "If I will that he tarry till I come, what is that to thee? follow thou me." Jesus told Peter that the main thing for him was not to have the future unveiled, but to do his present duty and faithfully follow Christ as His disciple. That is a word that is timely for all of us. There are many things about the present and many things about the future that we do not understand. Jesus here declared plainly, when He said, "till I come," that He would come again. There is no doubt about that. And what more impressive, what more tre-mendous fact can there be than that this same Jesus who talked with Peter and John and the rest of them, and who has filled history ever since, will one day come back to this earth? But the time of that coming He did not tell. Here at the very beginning He permitted some of His disciples to have a mis-taken idea about it. He could have told them plainly whether it was ten or a hundred or ten hundred years before He would come. But all that He said was, "If I will that John tarry till I come, what is that to thee?" And because He put it that way, although John did not take it so, many thought that Jesus meant that He was going to return to the earth before the death of John. No; we cannot be sure as to the time. Our duty is to do His will and ever be ready to meet Him, for as He said Himself, "Blessed are those servants, whom the lord when he cometh shall find watching. And if he shall come in the second watch or come in the third watch, and find them so, blessed are those servants."

There are many things in the Bible which we cannot now explain; there are deep questions about the Trinity, about the Atonement, about the fate of the heathen, about the terrible mass of wickedness and sorrow and pain that there is in the world today which we cannot answer. The best that we can do is to remember this: "The secret things belong unto the Lord our God: but those things which are revealed belong unto us and to our children for ever." There are some things the answer to which we must leave to God. For you and me the word is what Jesus spoke to Peter, "Follow me." That is always possible.

"Lovest thou me?" Why could Jesus ask Peter that question? Because He had suffered and died on the cross for Peter. Suppose Jesus had died a natural death at Bethany in the home of His friends, Mary and Martha and Lazarus? Suppose He had not knelt in Gethsemane or been scourged and spit upon and crowned with thorns and nailed to the cross by the Roman soldiers? Then how different would have been His question, "Lovest thou me?" Then our souls might well answer, "Lord, why should we love You?" and Jesus would have to be as silent and as speechless as the man in his own parable. But no; it is because He died on the cross and suffered for you that He can say to you what He said to Peter there by the glowing embers of that fire on Galilee's shore, "Lovest thou me?" What is your answer? Are you ready to say now what Peter did that morning, "Lord, thou knowest all things; thou knowest that I love thee"? And if you love Him, are you ready now to go forth as Peter did, forgetting the things that are behind, to follow Him and do His will and feed His sheep?

# 14

## WITH A CRIMINAL

Today shalt thou be with me in paradise (Luke 23:43).

I wish I had been there when that thief entered paradise, the first trophy of the Cross, the first fruits of the passion of Christ. It was a great day for the angels when Moses entered heaven, and David and Isaiah and John and Peter and Paul; but heaven has never seen such a day or heard such music as when the penitent thief passed through its gates.

"Bring out the prisoner!" In obedience to the gruff order of the centurion who was in command, the soldiers entered the guardhouse where they took from Jesus the crimson robe with which Herod had mocked Him and put on Him His own garment, that seamless robe which they looked upon with covetous eyes, wondering which one of them would possess it when the criminal who wore it had been crucified. In the prison were two other condemned men, robbers and murderers, awaiting execution of their sentence to death. Pilate thought he might as well get them out of the way at the time and instructed the centurion to crucify them together with Jesus.

A condemned man could not, of course, carry the heavy post upon which he was to be fastened, but it was the custom for him to carry the transom or the two planks which were to be nailed to the post and upon which his arms would be spread. These planks were laid upon the back of each one of the three condemned men, and the procession started toward Calvary.

Standing at the window of his palace, Pilate watched Jesus being led away with the cross upon His back. He gazed for a moment and then, turning away with a troubled look in his face, said to his wife Claudia, whose dream had warned him not to do that thing which now he could not undo, "An innocent man!"

In front of each criminal, according to the custom, marched a herald bearing a placard upon which was written the crime for which the man had been condemned to death. On the placards of the two thieves were the words, "Robber and Murderer," but on the placard in front of Jesus was the inscription in Latin, Greek, and Hebrew, so that everybody among the multitudes who were in Jerusalem at that time might read it and understand it, "Jesus of Nazareth, the King of the Jews." This was Pilate's scornful fling at the Jews; when the chief priests asked him to change it to, "He said, I am the King of the Jews," he roughly dismissed them, saying, "What I have written, I have written!"

Jerusalem at that time was filled with strangers who had come up to celebrate the Passover. The procession to Calvary went through the main street of the city so that all might see the criminals and be warned against a similar fate. As they passed along, the crowd fell in behind, eager to see the end of these dangerous men. Even the priests forgot their dignity and high office and walked along with the rabble mob, shouting their imprecations and cruel jests. The centurion marched imperiously ahead; the soldiers were on either side of the condemned men and behind them, sometimes roughly pushing the crowd aside and sometimes with their scourges and their curses urging the three men with the crosses on their backs to get along faster. In the crowd however, there were a few of the women who had known Jesus and loved Him. They followed after Him, weeping and wailing, their tears and their cries a strange contrast to the curses and blows of the soldiers and the jeers of the spectators.

Just as they were passing out of the gate of the city toward Golgotha, Jesus, weakened by the loss of blood through the brutal scourging which He had endured, stumbled and fell under His cross. Seeing that it was impossible for Him to carry it, the soldiers laid hold upon a proselyte Jew from North Africa, Simon of Cyrene, who had come up to celebrate the Passover and was standing in the line of march. They ordered him, much against his will, to take up the cross of Jesus and carry it for Him. We wonder if Simon said anything to Jesus as he walked by His side carrying His cross? And we wonder, too, if Jesus said anything to Simon? Did Simon get a glance from the face of Christ which touched his heart and, before they reached the Place of the Skull, made him glad that he had been able to help Him with His cross? Whether that was so or not, forever afterward Simon of Cyrene will be a name for those who in this world help Christ to bear His cross. So the procession passed on, out of the gate of the city and up the steep hill to the Place of the Skull.

When they had reached the well-known place of crucifixion, the condemned men were stripped of their clothing. The transverse planks were nailed to the post, and the doomed men were stretched upon them. Well hardened to the terrible duty, the soldiers went quickly and methodically about their tasks, driving nails through the hands of the prisoners, and then, drawing up their knees so that their feet were flat against the post, fastening the feet with spikes. Half way down the post was a peg known as the seat, which gave a degree of support to the body; otherwise the weight of the body would have torn it from the cross. Medicated wine was offered to the three men and partaken of by the two thieves, but not by Jesus. It was good for at least one of those thieves that Jesus did not partake of the opiate, for had He lost consciousness, the thief might never have heard those wonderful words, "Today shalt thou be with me in paradise."

## MOCKERY

When they saw Him at length lifted up on His cross there between the two thieves, the enemies of Jesus set up a great shout of exultation, and milling around the cross, coming as near to it as they dared, shaking their fists at Him and making sham obeisance before Him, they mocked the dying King of Grief. "Ha! destroyer of the temple and builder of it in three days, save Thyself and come down from the cross!" "He saved others, Himself He cannot save!" "If You are the Christ of God, His Chosen, then why does God not save You?" "You worked great miracles. Now give us one more miracle! You raised Lazarus from the grave; You restored the widow's son; You brought the daughter of the ruler back to life; now are You not able to save Yourself? You healed the woman with an issue of blood; why don't You stop the flow of Your own blood? You opened the eyes of the blind; You healed the paralytic; You cured ten lepers; why can't You do something for Yourself? Come on, now! Give us just one more miracle! Come down from the cross, and we will believe. One more miracle!" Even the soldiers, usually indifferent to the fate of men on the cross, got up from the ground where they were casting lots for His garments and began to mock Him, bowing grotesquely before Him, holding a cup of vinegar up to His lips and then withdrawing it from Him and shouting, "If you are the King of the Jews, as You say You are, why don't You save Yourself?"

In this chorus of mockery and execration, the two thieves at first joined their voices. Perhaps they had a faint hope that by thus joining in reviling Jesus they might gain at the last moment a reprieve. Or it may have been the natural explosion of tortured men and wicked hearts. Perhaps in the prison they had said one to another, "The time has come for us to die; but remember what we always vowed, that we will die cursing and blaspheming." So they cursed and mocked this ridiculous, naked king who hung between them; casting in his teeth all the jests and curses which they heard out of the mouths of the rulers, the priests, and the mob around the cross, and saying to Jesus, "If you are the Christ, save yourself and us! If you are a king, come down from the cross. Take us down with you, and then we will set up our kingdom. And what a kingdom that will be! Three kings—you and we two robbers!"

But now one of the thieves ceased to rail and mock. A new and strange look came over his distorted and agony-traced features. He was silent while the other robber went on taunting and reviling Jesus. Then, breaking his own silence, he called across the body of Jesus to his companion, "Be silent! Dost not thou fear God, seeing thou art in the same condemnation? And we indeed justly; for we receive the due reward of our deeds: but this man hath done nothing amiss." Again he was silent, while the other thief turned from mocking Jesus to mocking and taunting his fellow for his past crimes and his present change of heart. Then again breaking his silence and turning his head as far as the agony of the cross would permit, he looked toward the thorn-crowned head and prayed, "Lord, remember me when thou comest into thy kingdom." And with a sudden light flaming in His face Jesus answered, "Today shalt thou be with me in paradise."

This incomparable scene upon the cross—what the thief said to his fellow thief, what he said to Jesus, and what Jesus said to him—is the beautiful climax to the life and passion of Christ. Here is all the Gospel of repentance and faith and salvation.

REPENTANCE

The grace and miracle of repentance are explained and illustrated in the repentance of the dying robber. We do not know what agencies the Holy Spirit used to work the great change in the heart of that wicked and cruel man. Was it the taunts of the mob? Was it the way Jesus had claimed to be a king and said that He was the Son of God? Was it the sometimes softening effect of pain? Was it the beautiful prayer that he heard from the lips of Jesus, "Father, forgive them; for they know not what they do"? Was it what Jesus said to John about His mother and what He said to His mother about John? Did this strike a chord of tenderness in the memory of the heart of that poor robber? Or, perhaps, had he caught a look of pity and compassion from the eyes of the dying Savior? Whatever it was, the man's heart was changed. He repented of his sin.

It was a sincere and genuine repentance. That is proved by the fact that he confessed his sin. He confessed that he was an evildoer. He acknowledged, also, the righteousness and justice of the penalty which he was enduring, saying, "We indeed justly; for we receive the due reward of our deeds." He gave expression also to the fear of God, which grandly asserted itself in his soul in that dark and dreadful hour when he said to his fellow robber, "Dost not thou fear God?" That, too, showed the genuineness of his repentance, and repentance made him courageous, courageous enough to become a preacher to that companion with whom he had sinned and done wickedness for so many years. I can imagine the other thief turning on him, mocking him, and reviling him. "When did you turn preacher? You talk as if you had a better record than I have. Let me remind you of a few things. Do you remember that old merchant from Antioch whom you strangled for his gold and threw into the Orontes River? Do you remember that child that you stole from the villa at Tiberias and flung into the Jordan when we were closely pursued? Do you remember that young ruler whom you tortured and mutilated until he revealed to you the hiding place of his treasure? Do you remember that daughter of the captain of the guard whom you raped and defiled?" And so he went on through the catalog, the terrible catalog of the other robber's sins. Yet the penitent thief did not quail. He stuck to his sermon, "Dost not thou fear God? I know that you don't fear man. I learned that long ago. Neither do I. But what about God?"

## FAITH

The sublime faith of this thief is shown when he said to Jesus, "Lord, remember me when thou comest into thy kingdom." When you think of it, how marvelous an expression of faith that was—faith in the person of Christ, faith in the power of Christ, faith in the mercy of Christ, faith in the kingdom of Christ! His disciples who believed on Him during His life had His miracles to go by and the fulfillment of the prophecies; those who believe on Jesus today have the testimony of the Resurrection, the testimony of the Bible, the testimony of history, the testimony of the church through the ages. But this poor thief had none of those advantages. He had no prophet, no miracle, no resurrection from the dead; yet there he was, hanging on a cross in that dark and dreadful hour, putting his trust in the power and mercy and forgiving love of Jesus, coming to an understanding of the meaning of His death which Jesus had so often and so vainly sought to explain to His own disciples. It was the poor thief who first found the heart of the Gospel. In the naked man at his side, mocked, forsaken, crowned with thorns, His life blood ebbing rapidly away, the thief saw a king. He saw another crown than the crown of thorns, and he said, "Lord, when thou comest into thy kingdom, remember me. Give me a place in that kingdom."

How those words of the thief, that prayer of faith, that petition for mercy must have touched the heart of Christ, for it was to hear that prayer that Christ had come to die. "He saw the travail of his soul and was satisfied." Now let the thick darkness come down over the whole earth at the ninth hour. For him there was no darkness, for he had seen the everlasting light of redemption dawn upon a repentant soul. Now let the mob and the scribes and priests and Pharisees and soldiers and that other thief mock and jeer and curse. He heeded it not, for what he heard now was something else. It was a song that drowned out that chorus of shame and infamy, the song of heaven's angels rejoicing over one sinner that repents.

SALVATION

The end of repentance and faith is salvation. Here we can behold the salvation of a sinner. The thief had said, "Lord, remember me when thou comest into thy kingdom." Now Jesus broke that silence which no blow or taunt or curse of the cruel mob had been able to make Him break. The thief had said, "When thou comest," as if he were thinking of some far-off, remote age when Christ would set up His kingdom. Then, perhaps, he thought, Jesus would call him out of the sleep of death and give him a place in that kingdom. But to his eternal joy and surprise, Jesus answered, "Today shalt thou be with me in paradise!" The thief had asked only to be remembered. It was as if he had said, "Jesus, in thy kingdom I know that all the righteous will have a place and that there will be places of honor for the patriarchs and the prophets and for these Your twelve apostles. But in that day, O Lord, do not forget this poor thief who put his trust in You; show him some little portion, at least, of Your loving kindness and mercy." But

Jesus answered and said, "Today shalt thou be with me in paradise!" Immediately, at once, and first of all among those redeemed from sin after the death of Christ, he was to be admitted to paradise, the highest of the heavens—no obscure place in the suburbs of heaven, but in the very heart of it and at the very side of Jesus!

I wonder what the angels who were watching that great scene on the cross were thinking. Perhaps they had a debate as to who it should be that Jesus, having finished on the cross the work of redemption, would first admit to the kingdom of heaven. One angel was sure it would be the soul of Abraham, the father of the faithful, who saw his day and was glad. Another was sure it would be Moses, who wrote of Christ and talked with Him on the Mount of Transfiguration. Another was sure it would be Noah, who, when all the earth was corrupt before God, feared God and served Him. Another was sure it would be David, great in his sin and great in his repentance, who had sung the splendors of Christ's everlasting kingdom. And others were certain that it would be Isaiah, the evangelical prophet who, long before Christ came and died, described him as a man of sorrows and acquainted with grief, numbered with the transgressors, bruised for our iniquities, and wounded for our transgressions. And still another was sure that the soul who would enter heaven first with Christ would be John the Baptist, the first of all to hail Jesus as the Lamb of God that takes away the sins of the world. But now their debate and speculation came to an end, for a sentinel on the outposts of heaven reported that the Son of God, having led captivity captive, was on His way home and that before long they would see who it was that Christ would bring first into heaven. It was not Abraham or Moses or David or Isaiah or John the Baptist. No; none of these. Lo, Christ came, and with Him He brought the soul of a penitent thief! And when the Father on the throne beheld him, He cried out, "Bring forth the best robe, and put it on him; and put a ring on his hand, and shoes on his feet: for this my son was dead, and is alive again; he was lost and is found."

There is only one way to heaven, and that is the way the penitent thief traveled. There is only one gate into heaven, and that is the gate through which the penitent thief entered, the gate of repentance toward God and faith in the Lord Jesus Christ. That gate is open today for you and for me. "If thou shalt confess with thy mouth the Lord Jesus, and shalt believe in thine heart that God hath raised Him from the dead, thou shalt be saved."

# 15

## WITH A MAN ON AN ISLAND

And heard behind me a great voice, as of a trumpet (Rev. 1:10).

And the echo of that trumpet voice still rolls down the ages. The stars were shining brightly in the unclouded canopy of heaven. Noiselessly the ship glided into a landlocked harbor and then, with a rattling of the anchor chains, came to a standstill. Looking over the rail of the ship, I could see the dim outline of mountains. A small boat put off from the side of the steamer, and we were rowed into the landing place. The stars now were beginning to pale, and the sun, rising over the sea to the east, lit up the tops of the mountain and turned the waters into a sea of glass mingled with fire. Far up on top of the mountains appeared the white buildings of the eleven-hundred-year-old monastery of St. John. Absolute silence reigned. Silence on the sea. Silence on the land. Deep silence, like that which was in heaven for half an hour when the seventh seal of the Apocalypse was opened. And such a silence, I thought, was a fit introduction to that immortal isle, for that is where we were standing now, on "the isle that is called Patmos."

John was one of the two disciples, John and James, who asked for a seat at the right hand of Christ in the glory of His kingdom. Jesus told them that they understood not what they were asking. But when I get to heaven there are three men whom I expect to see not far from the throne—Paul and Peter and John. To John it was granted to see the glory of heaven and the kingdom of God and to write what he had seen.

John's acquaintance with Jesus began that memorable day by the Jordan when he heard the Baptist say of Jesus as He passed by, "Behold the Lamb of God." John could never forget that hour. Writing perhaps half a century after, he remembered all the circumstances, just who were present and what was said and the very hour of the day, just how high the sun was over the horizon to the west, for he says, "It was about the tenth hour." John had other great hours with Jesus: when he saw Him transfigured in glory on the mount, when he saw Him die on the cross and heard Him cry, "It is finished," when he saw Him in the morning of the Resurrection, when he saw Him at the Mount of Olives as He ascended into heaven and lifted His hands in blessing upon the disciples, and when he saw Him here on Patmos standing in the midst of the seven golden candlesticks with the seven stars in His right hand; but the greatest hour in John's life was that tenth hour when he first knew Christ as his Lord and Savior. And that ever should be the great hour in the history of an immortal soul.

It is well established that John spent a good part of his life and ministry in the great city of Ephesus. Polycarp, who was burned to death for the sake of Christ at Smyrna, left behind him the record of John's teaching and preaching at Ephesus. There are interesting traditions about John and his ministry in that city. One tells how, when one of his converts had backslidden and joined a band of robbers and brigands, John followed him to the mountain den of the robbers and wept over him and prayed over him until he won him back to Christ. When he was too old and too feeble to walk or to preach, John used to have himself carried into the assembly of the Christians and there, lifting his hands in benediction, would say to them, "Little children, love one another." But John could be stern, too, as we know from his letters, toward unbelievers. There were times when he was a son of thunder. Once he hurried from a public bath where he had met the heretic Cerinthus who denied that God had come in the flesh in Christ, for he feared, he said, that the roof would fall on him.

Sometime during his ministry at Ephesus, probably under

the reign of the Emperor Domitian, John, as a follower of Christ, was exiled to the Isle of Patmos and sentenced to hard labor in the lead mines or the quarries on that island. Patmos is a tiny island some sixty miles off the coast of Asia Minor. The island is only ten miles long, and in the middle of it, where the fort is, it narrows almost to an isthmus. The mountains rise to a height of eight hundred feet. It was a fitting stage for the great vision. Although so near to the mainland of Asia, where so much of the world's history has been made, the island has the atmosphere of complete detachment and remoteness from the tides of the world's busy life. After a few days on Patmos one begins to understand the imagery and the metaphors of the Apocalypse. The sea dominates everything else; John mentions the sea in the Apocalypse twenty-five times, both as a place of glory and as an agent of separation and sorrow. Coming down from the monastery and the grotto where John is supposed to have had his great dream, we paused on an ancient bridge to view the sinking sun. In a moment it had touched the westward sea, and there, just as John saw it when he beheld the redeemed standing on it and singing the song of Moses and the Lamb, was a "sea of glass, mingled with fire."

THE VISION

In prison on this isle called Patmos for the Word of God and the testimony of Jesus Christ, John, in the Spirit on the Lord's Day, heard behind him a great voice as of a trumpet. When he turned to see who it was that spoke with him, he saw standing in the midst of seven golden candlesticks one like unto the Son of Man, His head and His hair white like wool, as white as snow; in His right hand He had seven stars, out of His mouth went a sharp, two-edged sword. John fell at His feet as one dead. But Christ lifted him up, telling him not to be afraid, that He was the first and the last, Alpha and Omega, and that He had the keys of death and of hell. John was then told to write the things which he was to see and to hear. And what John wrote is the great Apocalypse, the book of Revelation.

This interview with John is the last of the interviews of Jesus. What John heard in this interview, therefore, is the last message of Christ to the believer. Not until Christ comes again will He speak with man as He spoke with John on that island. When Jesus predicted the martyr's death for Peter, and Peter impulsively asked what was going to happen to John, Jesus answered, "If I will that he tarry till I come, what is that to thee?" John, in his account of that meeting with Christ and Peter there by the Sea of Galilee, makes it clear that Jesus did not definitely say that John was to live until Christ came again. And yet, in a certain sense, one might say that John did tarry until Jesus came, for he was permitted to see the scroll of the future unrolled and in great principle at least, the whole history of the church and of the world until Christ shall come in glory.

Let us take our stand, then, upon this mountain of vision and revelation, and with the book of Revelation in our hand, invoking the aid of the Holy Spirit and the spirit of John, too, let us see what John saw, "I looked, and, behold, a door was opened in heaven." Looking through the door, John saw the throne of God, like a jasper and a sardine stone with a rainbow round about it. Before the throne and before Him who sat upon the throne four and twenty elders fell down in worship, and four mysterious creatures full of eyes constantly sang praises to the Creator of the world. Then followed in quick and overwhelming succession the great signs and wonders: the sealed book, inscrutable to mortals and angels, being loosed by the Lamb of God; the seven seals being broken one after the other, with the judgments following each one; the stars falling and the mountains quaking; silence on the sea and silence on the land and silence in heaven for the space of half an hour; then the seven angels sounding on their seven trumpets; the great battle between the followers of the Lamb and the followers of Satan; the dragon pursuing the woman and her child; the beast with his death stroke healed; the seven angels with the seven vials of judgment; the war of the dragon; the victory of the Lamb; the white horse and his Rider; and then the Holy City, the New Jerusalem, coming down from God out of heaven, like a bride adorned for her husband. The history of mankind was finished. The kingdom of Satan was overthrown, and the kingdoms of this world were become the kingdoms of our Lord and of His Christ.

That, in brief, is what John saw and heard on the isle that is called Patmos. But what do these strange scenes, these dreadful beasts, these flaming signs, these glorious walls and temples, these bursts of heavenly music—what do they mean to you and me today? What of profit and of inspiration, of warning and of hope, is there for you and me in this momentous interview of Jesus with John?

## THE MAJESTY AND PREEMINENCE OF CHRIST

The Apocalypse is a cyclorama of history, a photograph of the ages, past, present, and to come; and over all the ages towers in majesty the glory the Son of God. Christ is the preeminent figure in time and eternity. Amid all these overwhelming scenes which meet our eyes when we open the pages of the Apocalypse, amid all these strange, glorious, and sometimes terrible personalities and forces and powers which appear in the Apocalypse, Christ towers supreme. Beasts, dragons, devils, confederated powers of darkness, all the hosts of Satan go down before Him to everlasting ruin and destruction.

This is a new Christ whom John sees standing on Patmos amid the seven golden candlesticks; yet He is the same Christ, for He is the same yesterday, today, and forever. When Jesus was on earth in the days of His flesh, John had leaned on His breast at the supper. But now when the Beloved Disciple beholds Him standing there in the midst of the seven golden candlesticks with the seven stars in His right hand, His countenance flaming like the sun and out of His mouth proceeding a sharp, two-edged sword, and His voice like the sound of many waters, John falls in terror at His feet as one that is dead. Here is the Christ who is the Ruler of the ages, who will break the nations like a potter's vessel; here is the Christ who directs the movements of history. He is the Christ who is the Alpha and Omega, the beginning and the end. He is the Christ who says, "I have the keys of hell and of death." The politicians and the statesmen, even the best and the most high-minded of them, do not have the keys. Education does not have the keys. Science, the knowledge of the natural world, does not have the keys. But Christ, who was dead and is alive and who liveth forevermore, holds the keys.

Is the world on the verge of a great change and breakup and catastrophe? Are the last times at hand? Who knows? In certain respects it would seem that every scheme and plan and system of government, of education, of organization has been tried and found wanting. But whatever lies in the future, we know that Christ has the keys, that history has begun and will end in Him, that all proceeds according to the divine plan, that He is Alpha and Omega, the beginning and the end.

In this preeminent and glorious Christ, the preeminent fact is His death on the cross, His atonement for the sins of men. The music of the great book opens with a grand overture to the Christ of Calvary: "Unto him that loved us, and washed us from our sins in his own blood, and hath made us kings and priests unto God and his Father; to him be glory and dominion forever and ever. Amen." It is the slain Lamb who looses the seven seals of the book of the world's destiny. It is the Lamb standing upon Mount Zion, slain from the foundations of the world, who leads the battle against the enemies of God. The light of the Eternal City is the light of the Lamb. The water of the Eternal City is the river of the water of life that flows from the throne of the Lamb. The final and deciding fact in the destinies of the world and in the war between good and evil is the Cross of Jesus Christ.

## STRUGGLE BETWEEN GOOD AND EVIL

Here we behold all the unbelief, all the apostasies, all the conspiracies, all the rebellions against God, all the persecutions of Christ and His church. But this battle issues in final and overwhelming victory. When the sixth angel, after the seven angels had sounded on their trumpets, poured out his vial upon the waters and upon the earth, the infernal trinity, the beast and the dragon and the false prophet, went forth to make war upon Christ and His followers. But when this battle was over, the seventh angel poured out his vial into the air and there came a voice out of the temple of heaven from the throne, saying, "It is done!" The great prophetic cry of Christ when

He expired in the darkness of Calvary, "It is finished," is answered now by the cry of triumph, "It is done!" Then heaven is opened, and the white horse and His Rider, many crowns on His head and His vesture dipped in blood, go forth conquering and to conquer.

## THE NEW JERUSALEM

The great book comes to a close with the sublime picture of the New Jerusalem coming down from God out of heaven like a bride adorned for her husband. John has two masterpieces which deal with the heavenly life. One is in his gospel where he relates that precious fragment from the interview of Jesus with His disciples, John resting his head upon His breast, on the same night in which the Master was betrayed, "Let not your heart be troubled: ye believe in God, believe also in me. In my Father's house are many mansions." The other is this final passage from the Apocalypse, where John was permitted to see what those mansions are like, the home which is curseless, tearless, sinless, painless, and deathless. Yes; until we see no longer through the glass darkly, but face-to-face, and until the veil is rent, this sweet music of John where he describes the Holy City will best voice our hopes and expectations for the life which is to come.

This grand goal of the human race, this divine consummation to the drama of human history, is brought about by no human power, by no slow evolution and development of human society, but by the triumphant and glorious advent of the Son of God Himself. Hence the book closes with the assurance of the mighty Christ who appears in its pages, "Behold, I come quickly!" And answering to that is the inspired prayer of John and the prayer of the church wherever it follows the Lamb of God, wherever it exalts the redeeming power of His Cross, wherever it waits for the coming of His kingdom: "Even so, come, Lord Jesus!"

Books by Clarence E. Macartney

*Chariots of Fire*
*The Faith Once Delivered*
*Great Women of the Bible*
*The Greatest Questions of the Bible and of Life*
*The Greatest Texts of the Bible*
*The Greatest Words in the Bible and in Human Speech*
*He Chose Twelve*
*The Parables of the Old Testament*
*Parallel Lives of the Old and New Testaments*
*Paul the Man*
*The Prayers of the Old Testament*
*Strange Texts but Grand Truths*
*Twelve Great Questions About Christ*